Help Me! Guide to the G--g-- --xel

By Charles Hughes

Getting Started

Table of Contents

1. Button Layout

The Pixel has two buttons and two jacks. The touchscreen is used to control all functions on the Pixel, with the exception of turning the phone on and off and adjusting the volume. The Pixel has the following buttons and jacks:

Back Key Home Key Overview Key

Figure 1: Front View

On-Screen Navigation Keys - The navigation keys described below respond to your touch. Touch each key on the screen to perform the corresponding action:

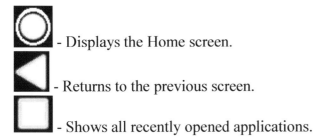

- Displays the Home screen.

- Returns to the previous screen.

- Shows all recently opened applications.

Figure 2: Rear View

Fingerprint Scanner - Allows you to unlock your phone and use certain applications to pay for goods or log in to your account.

Figure 3: Top View

Headphone Jack - Allows headphones to be connected to the phone.

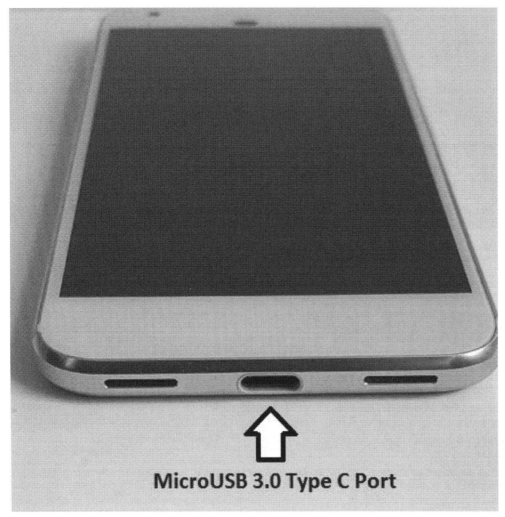

MicroUSB 3.0 Type C Port

Figure 4: Bottom View

MicroUSB 3.0 Type C Port - Connects the phone to a computer or to a charger.

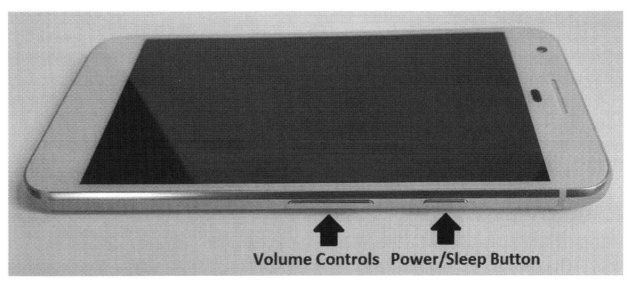

Figure 5: Right Side View

Power/Sleep Button - Turns the phone on and off or puts the phone to sleep.
Volume Controls - Increases and decreases the media volume.

Figure 6: Left Side View

SIM Card Slot - Stores the SIM card for your phone. Transfer a SIM card from an old phone to keep your phone number and your network provider. When you transfer a SIM card, nothing changes on your mobile plan other than the type of phone that you are using.

2. Charging the Phone

To charge the phone, use the included charging adapter to plug the phone in to a power outlet. Chargers that come with other Android phones, such as the Samsung Galaxy or HTC One, are not compatible with the Pixel. Do not use a USB port on a computer, as it may not charge the phone fully. To charge the phone while it is turned off, simply plug it in. The phone will not turn itself on when it is plugged in to a power source.

3. Turning the Phone On and Off

To turn the phone on, press and hold the **Power** button for three seconds or until 'Google' appears. The phone takes several moments to start up.

To turn the phone off, press and hold the **Power** button until 'Power Off' appears. Touch **Power off**. The phone turns off.

4. Waking Up Your Phone

There are several ways in which you can interact with the lock screen. Refer to the following tips when controlling your phone from the lock screen:

- Touch the screen and move your finger up to unlock the phone.

- Touch the icon and move your finger up to turn on the camera.

- Touch the icon and move your finger to the right to open the Phone application.

- Touch the screen and move your finger down to view notifications and the current weather.

Note: You can bypass the lock screen entirely by setting the Screen Lock to **None**. *Refer to* "Leaving the Screen Unlocked at All Times" *on page 259 to learn how.*

5. Navigating the Screens

There are many ways to navigate the phone. These are a few of the methods:

- Use the 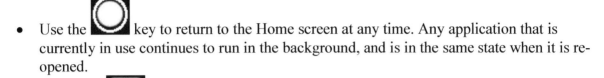 key to return to the Home screen at any time. Any application that is currently in use continues to run in the background, and is in the same state when it is re-opened.

- Touch the key to view all recently opened applications. Touch an application in the list to switch to it. Refer to *"Viewing Recently Opened Applications"* on page 115 to learn more.

- While viewing a Home screen, slide your finger to the left or right to access additional Home screens.

- Touch the key at any time to return to the previous screen or menu.

- Touch the key while using the keyboard to hide it.

6. Types of Home Screen Objects

Each Home screen on the phone is fully customizable. Refer to *"Organizing Home Screen Objects"* on page 17 to learn how to customize the Home screens. Each screen can hold the following items:

- **Widget** - A tool that can be used directly on the Home screen without opening it like an application. Widgets usually take up a fraction or all of the screen, while applications are added as icons. The Weather widget is shown in **Figure 7**.
- **Application** - A program that opens in a new window, such as Gmail or a game. Applications are added to the Home screen as icons.
- **Folder** - A folder of application icons or shortcuts.

Note: A folder cannot store widgets.

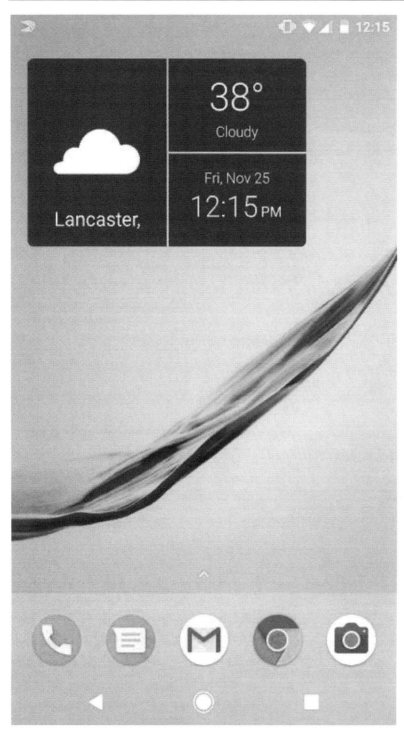

Figure 7: Weather Widget

7. Organizing Home Screen Objects

Customize the Home screens by adding, deleting, or moving objects. Refer to *"Types of Home Screen Objects"* on page 15 to learn more about them. To add an object to a Home screen:

1. Touch the bottom of any Home screen and slide your finger up. A list of all installed applications appears, as shown in **Figure 8**.

2. Touch and hold an application icon and begin moving your finger. The Home screen that you were previously viewing appears.

3. Release the screen. The object is placed in the selected location on the Home screen.

To add a widget, touch and hold an empty space on a home screen, then touch **Widgets**. Follow steps 2-3 above to learn how to add the widget to the selected Home screen.

Note: If you are returned to the home screen, then you have tried to place the object on a Home screen that does not have sufficient space. Refer to the following hints to learn how to create space on a Home screen.

There are multiple ways to clean up the Home screens. Use the following tips to create space on Home screens:

- To remove an object from the Home screen, touch and hold the object until **Remove** appears at the top of the screen. Move the object over **Remove** and release the screen. The object is removed from the Home screen. It is still installed on the phone, and will continue to appear in the list of installed applications. Refer to *"Uninstalling an Application"* on page 109 to learn how to remove an application from your phone.
- To move an object, touch and hold it until **Remove** appears at the top of the screen. Move the object to the desired location and release the screen to place it. Move the object to the edge of the screen to move it to another Home screen.
- To create a folder, touch and hold an application icon, and drag it on top of another. To add more icons to an existing folder, drag the icons on top of the existing folder. To remove an icon from a folder, touch and hold it, drag it anywhere outside the folder, and release the screen. When only one icon remains in a folder, the folder is automatically deleted and the remaining icon is returned to the Home screen.

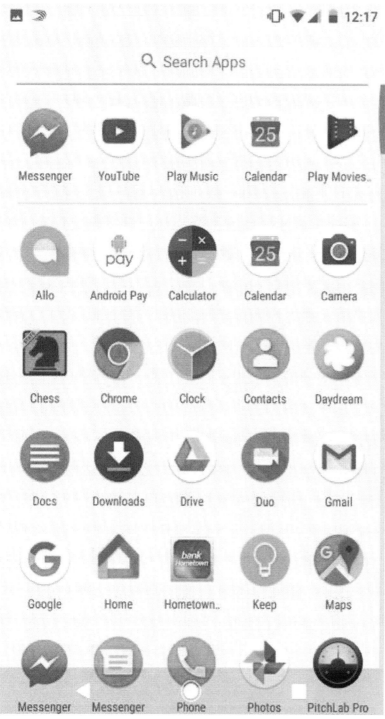

Figure 8: List of All Installed Applications

8. Exporting and Importing Files Using a PC or Mac

You can import files, such as images and documents, to the phone from a computer. You can also export files from the phone to a computer. To export and import files using a PC or Mac:

1. Connect the phone to your PC or Mac using the provided USB cable. If you are using a Mac, download the Android File Transfer application at **www.android.com/filetransfer/** before proceeding.
2. Unlock the phone, then touch the top of the screen and slide your finger down. Touch **USB charging this device**. The Use USB to window appears, as shown in **Figure 9**.
3. Touch **Transfer Files**. You are now ready to export and import files.

4. Double-click the ![icon] icon in the Computer folder, as outlined in **Figure 10**, if using a PC. On a Mac, open the Android File Transfer program. The phone folder opens. To access the Computer folder on a PC, click the ![button] button and then click **Computer** in Windows Vista or later. Double-click **My Computer** on the desktop in Windows 95 or later.
5. Double-click **Internal shared storage**. The Internal shared storage folder opens on a PC, as shown in **Figure 11**, or on a Mac, as shown in **Figure 12**.
6. Double-click a folder inside the Internal Storage folder to view its contents. The folder opens.
7. Click and drag a file into the folder from your computer, or drag one to your computer from the phone folder. The file is transferred.

Note: Operating systems prior to Windows Vista may not be able to recognize the phone when it is connected. The image below is for a Pixel, and will vary based on the phone that you use.

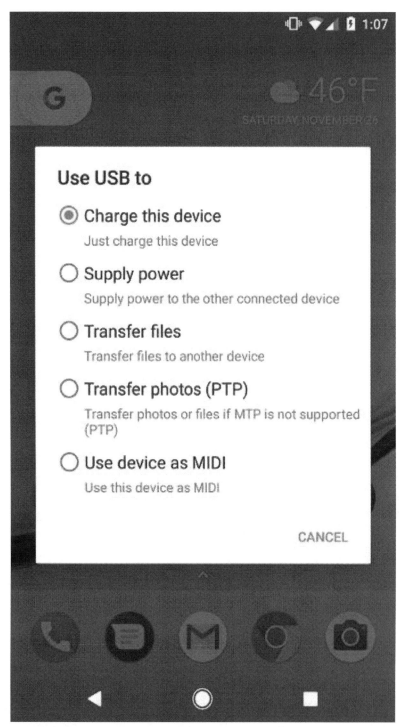

Figure 9: Use USB To Window

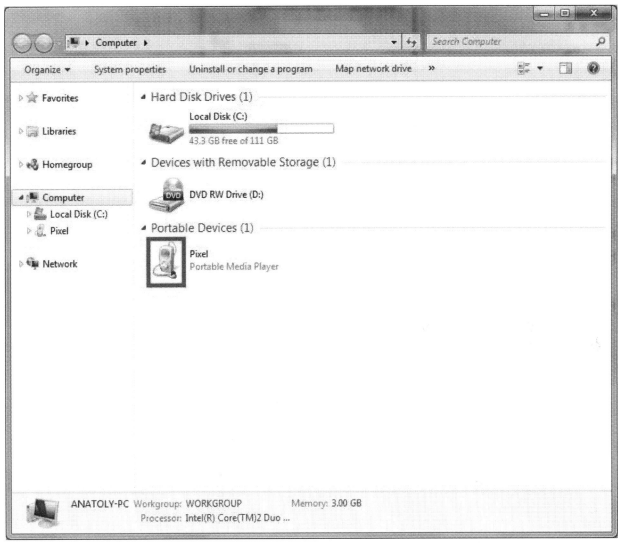

Figure 10: Pixel Icon on a PC

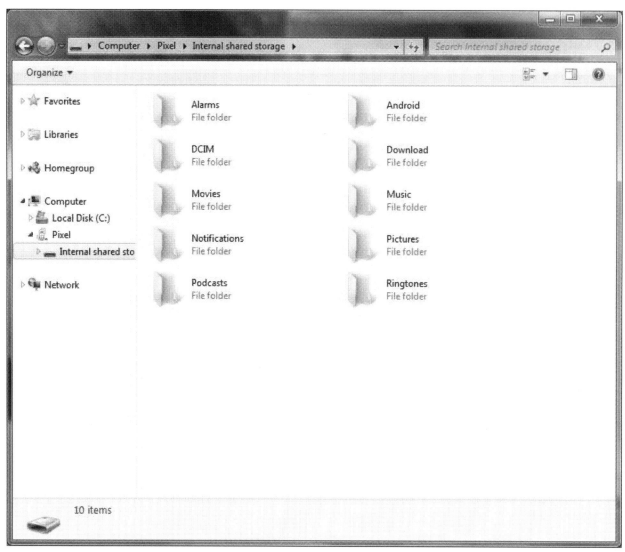

Figure 11: Internal Storage Folder on a PC

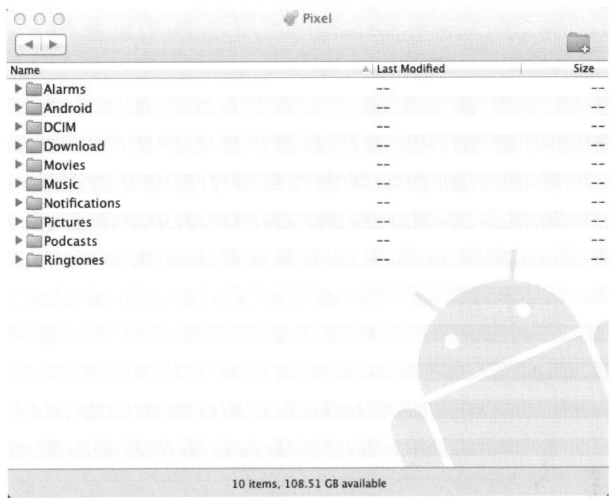

Figure 12: Internal Storage Folder on a Mac

9. Working with Notifications

There are several new features surrounding notifications in Android Lollipop. Refer to the following tips when working with notifications:

1. **Interacting with Lock Screen Notifications** - You can interact with notifications that appear on the lock screen in several ways. For example, if you touch a notification and slide your finger down, you are sometimes presented with options, such as to reply to or archive an email. You can also touch a notification twice to open the application that sent it.
2. **Managing Status Bar Notifications** - When the phone is unlocked and you receive a notification, you can do one of three things:
3. Touch the notification to open the application that sent it.

4. Touch the application and slide your finger to the left or right to clear the notification.
5. Touch **Reply** to respond to a text message quickly without opening the Messenger application.

Allowing Notifications in Do Not Disturb Mode - Do Not Disturb mode blocks all notifications except for alarms. When Do Not Disturb mode is turned on, only those applications that you have given priority can send you notifications. To customize Do Not Disturb mode:

1. Touch the bottom of any Home screen and slide your finger up. A list of all installed applications appears
2. Touch **Settings**. The Settings screen appears, as shown in **Figure 13**.
3. Touch **Notifications**. The Notifications screen appears, as shown in **Figure 14**.
4. Touch an application in the list. The App Notifications screen appears, as shown in **Figure 15**.
5. Touch **Override Do Not Disturb**. The application is now allowed to send you notifications when in Do Not Disturb mode.

To turn on Do Not Disturb mode:

1. Touch the top of the screen with two fingers and slide down. The Quick Settings appear, as shown in **Figure 16**.
2. Touch **Do Not Disturb**. The Do not disturb screen appears, as shown in **Figure 17**.
3. Touch one of the following options:
   - **Total silence -** Mutes all sounds, including alarms.
   - **Alarms Only** - Mutes all sounds except for alarms.
   - **Priority Only** - Mutes all sounds except for notifications from Priority applications.
4. Touch **Until you turn this off** or **For one hour** to schedule Do Not Disturb.
5. Touch **Done**. Do Not Disturb is turned on. To turn off Do Not Disturb, touch **Do not disturb** in the Notification options.

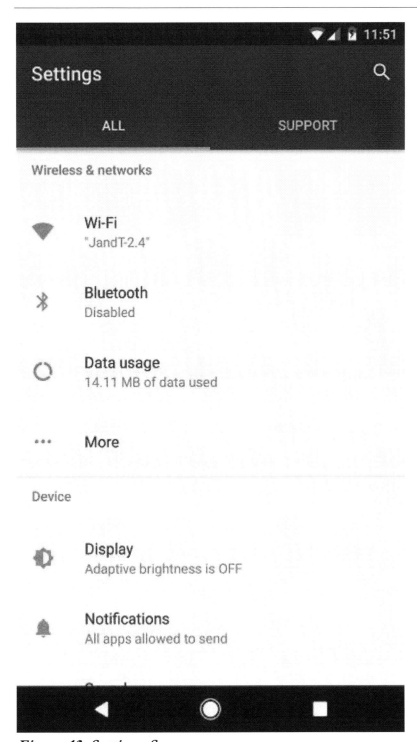

Figure 13: Settings Screen

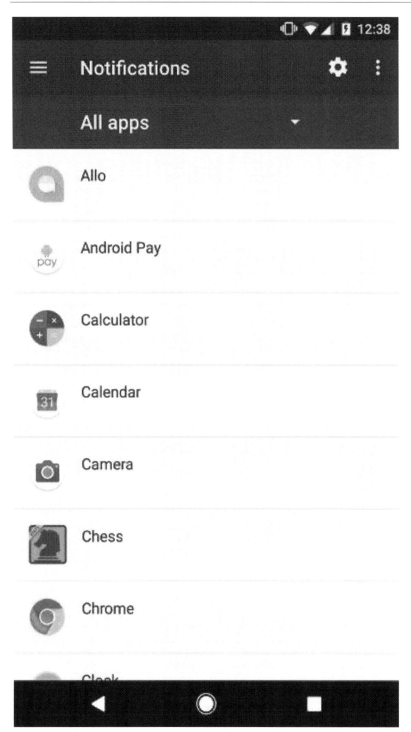

Figure 14: Notifications Screen

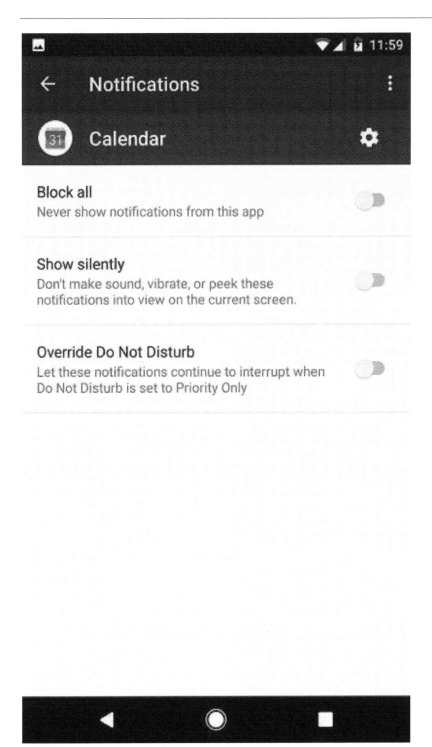

Figure 15: App Notifications Screen

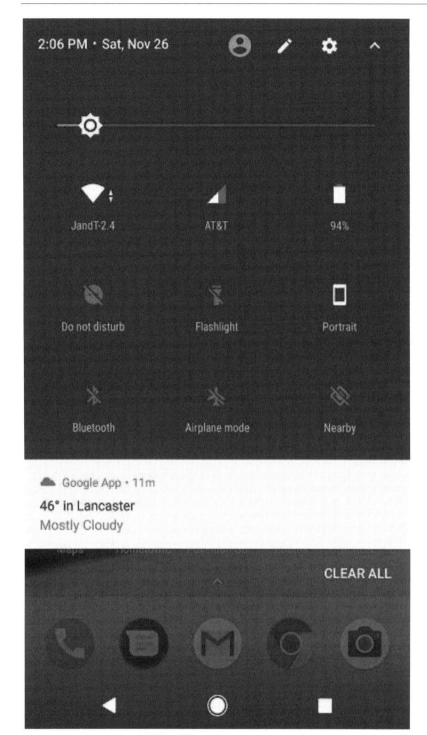

Figure 16: Notification Options

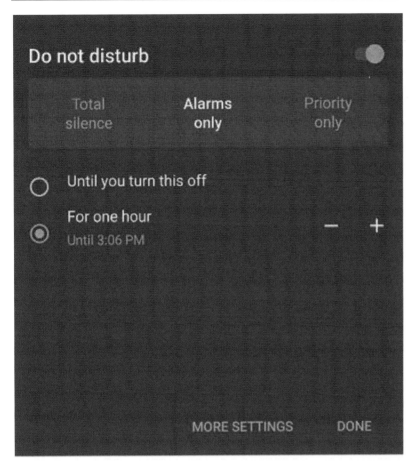

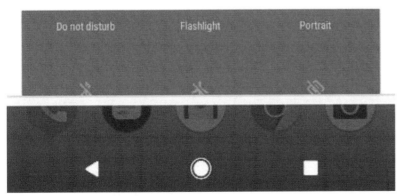

Figure 17: Do Not Disturb Screen

Making Calls

Table of Contents

1. Dialing a Number

Numbers that are not in your phonebook can be dialed on the keypad. To manually dial a phone number:

1. Touch the icon at the bottom of the screen. The Favorites screen appears, as shown in **Figure 1**.

2. Touch the icon at the bottom of the screen. The Keypad appears, as shown in **Figure 2**.

3. Enter a phone number and touch the button at the bottom of the screen. The phone calls the number.

Figure 1: Favorites Screen

Figure 2: Phone Keypad

2. Calling a Contact

If a number is stored in your Phonebook, you may touch the name of a contact to dial the number. Refer to *"Adding a New Contact"* on page 177 to learn how to add a contact to the Phonebook. To call a contact who is already stored in your Phonebook:

1. Touch the icon at the bottom of the screen. The Speed Dial screen appears.
2. Touch the icon at the top of the screen. The Phonebook appears, as shown in **Figure 3**.
3. Touch a contact's name. The Contact Information screen appears, as shown in **Figure 4**.
4. Touch the number that you wish to call. The phone dials the number.

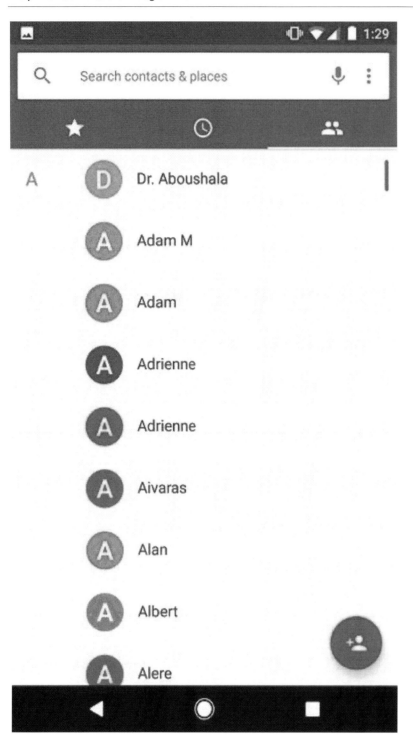

Figure 3: Phonebook

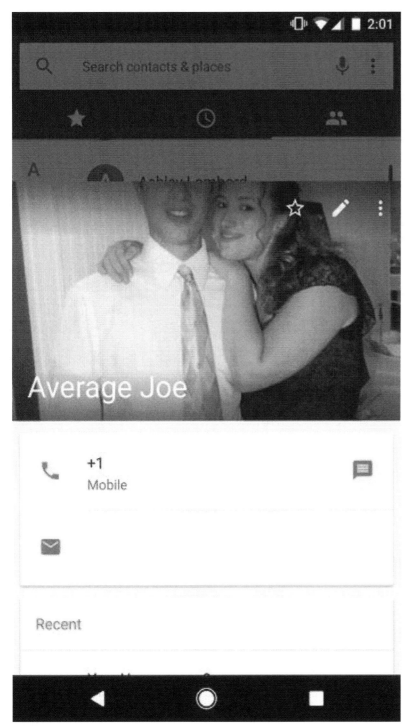

Figure 4: Contact Information Screen

3. Calling a Frequently Dialed Number

You can add a Direct Dial shortcut to the Home screen, which immediately dials a number that is stored in your phonebook when you touch the shortcut. To add and use a Direct Dial shortcut:

1. Touch an empty space on the home screen. The Home screen editing menu appears, as shown in **Figure 5**.
2. Touch **Widgets** at the bottom of the screen. A list of widgets appears, as shown in **Figure 6**.

3. Scroll down to find the Direct Dial widget under the **Contacts** section. Touch the icon and drag it to the desired location on the Home screen. The Phonebook appears.

4. Touch the number that you would like to assign to the direct dial. The Direct Dial shortcut is set and appears on the Home screen, as shown in **Figure 7**.
5. Touch the **Direct Dial** icon. The number is dialed.

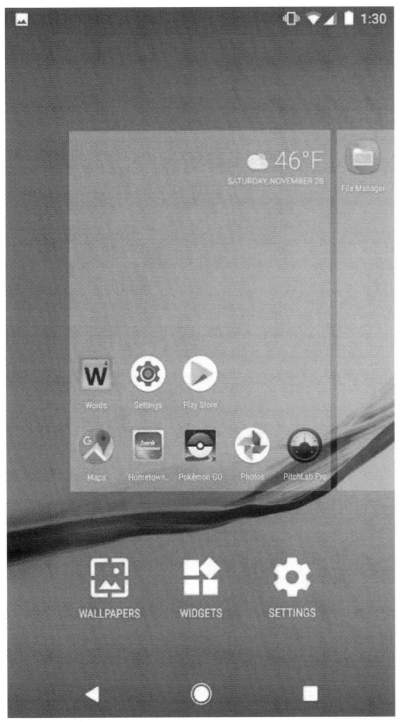

Figure 5: Home Screen Editing Menu

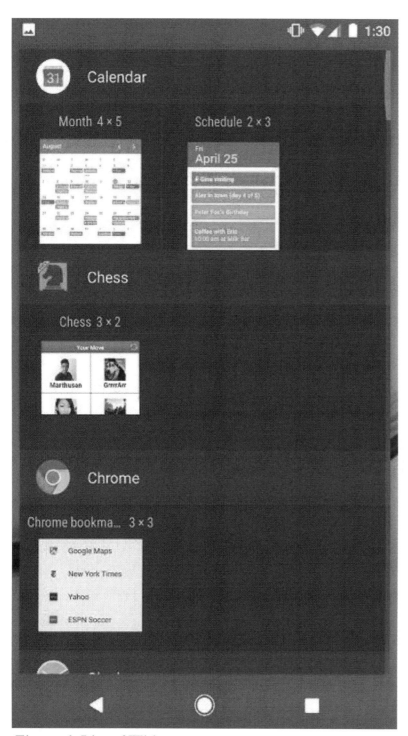

Figure 6: List of Widgets

Figure 7: Direct Dial Icon on the Home Screen

4. Returning a Recent Phone Call

After you miss a call, the phone notifies you of who called and at what time. The phone also shows a history of all recent calls. To view and return a missed call or redial a recently entered number:

1. Touch the  icon at the bottom of the screen. The Speed Dial screen appears.

2. Touch the 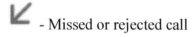 icon. A list of recent calls appears, as shown in **Figure 8**. The following indicators appears next to the calls:

   - Received call

   - Missed or rejected call

3. Touch the icon next to the name of a contact. The phone calls the selected contact.

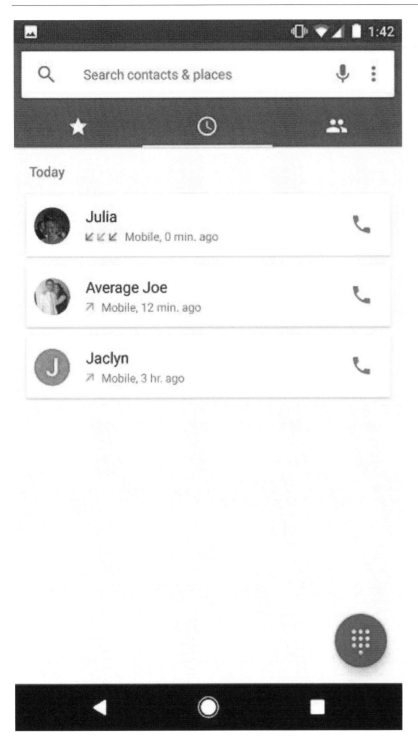

Figure 8: List of Recent Calls

5. Receiving a Voice Call

When receiving a voice call with the screen locked, the Incoming Call Lock Screen appears, as shown in **Figure 9**. To answer the call, touch the contact's picture and drag it up. The call is connected. To decline the call, touch the contact's picture and drag it down. The call is sent to voicemail.

If the screen is unlocked, a pop-up appears at the top of the screen, as shown in **Figure 10**. Touch **Answer** to answer the call, or touch **Decline** to reject it.

You can also respond to a phone call using a text message from the lock screen by sliding the icon up.

Figure 9: Incoming Call Screen

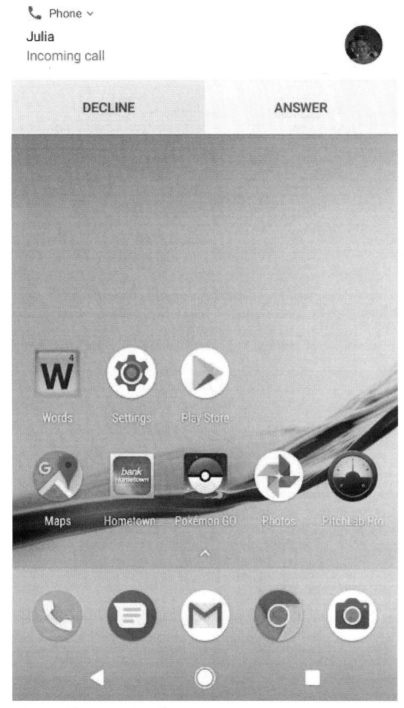

Figure 10: Incoming Call Popup

6. Using the Speakerphone During a Voice Call

The Pixel has a built-in Speakerphone, which is useful when calling from a car or when several people need to participate in a conversation. To use the speakerphone during a phone call:

1. Place a phone call. The Calling Screen appears, as shown in **Figure 11**.

2. Touch the ◀ icon. The speakerphone turns on.

3. Adjust the volume of the Speakerphone using the Volume Controls. Refer to *"Button Layout"* on page 7 to locate the Volume Controls.

4. Touch the ◀ icon again. The speakerphone turns off.

Figure 11: Calling Screen

7. Using the Keypad during a Voice Call

You may wish to use the keypad while on a call in order to input numbers in an automated menu or to enter an account number. To use the keypad during a voice call, place the call and touch the icon. The keypad appears, as shown in **Figure 12**. To hide the keypad, touch the icon again.

Figure 12: Phone Keypad While on a Call

8. Using the Mute Function during a Voice Call

During a voice call, you may wish to mute your side of the conversation. When mute is turned on, the person on the other end of the line will not hear anything on your side. To use Mute during a

call, place a voice call and touch the icon. The phone mutes your voice and the caller(s) can

no longer hear you, but you are still able to hear them. Touch the icon again. Mute is turned off.

9. Starting a Conference Call (Adding a Call)

To talk to more than one person at a time, place a new call without ending the current one. To add a call:

1. Place a call. The call is connected and the Calling screen appears.

2. Touch the icon. The keypad appears.

3. Dial a number and touch the button or touch the name of the contact. The phone dials the second number.

4. Touch the icon once the second call is connected. The calls are merged and a three-person conference call is started.

10. Redialing the Last Dialed Number

You may redial the number that you last dialed by touching the button at the bottom of the

phone keypad. The last dialed number appears above the keypad. Touch the button again. The number is redialed.

11. Making a Video Call

You can use the Duo application that comes pre-installed on the Pixel to make video calls. To set up the application, you will need to agree to the terms and conditions and verify your phone number.

To make a video call using duo, touch the icon, then touch **Video call**, as shown in **Figure 13**. The phonebook appears. Touch the name of a contact to place a video call.

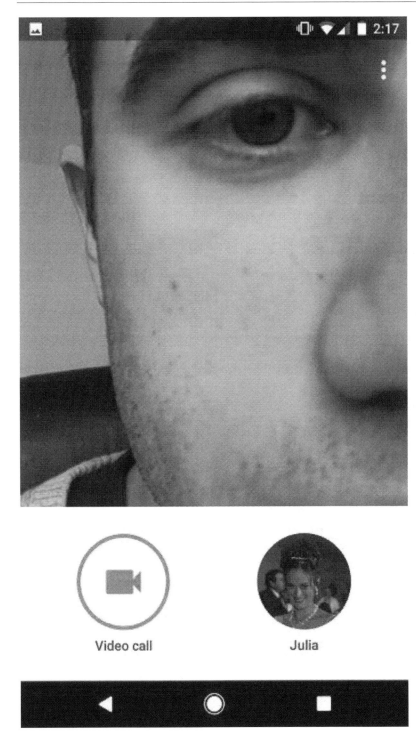

Figure 13: Duo Application

Text Messaging

Table of Contents

1. Composing a New Text Message

Your phone can send text messages to other mobile phones. To compose a new text message:

1. Touch the [icon] icon at the bottom of the Home screen. The Messaging screen appears, as shown in **Figure 1**.

2. Touch the [icon] icon. The New Message screen appears, as shown in **Figure 2**. A list of frequently contacted people appears.

3. Touch the name of a contact in the list, or enter a phone number. Suggestions appear while typing. The addressee or phone number is entered.

4. Touch the [icon] key on the keyboard. A new conversation with the selected contact is created.

5. Enter a message, and touch the [icon] button. The message is sent and appears as a conversation, sorted by send date, as shown in **Figure 3**.

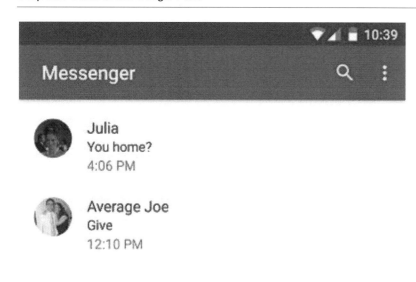

Julia
You home?
4:06 PM

Average Joe
Give
12:10 PM

Figure 1: Messaging Screen

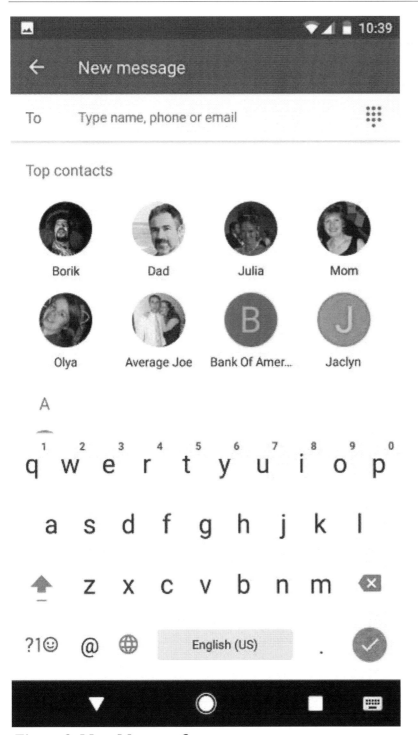

Figure 2: New Message Screen

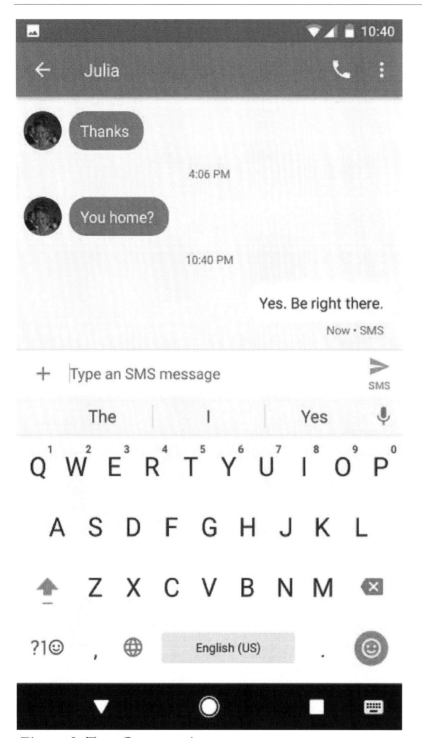

Figure 3: Text Conversation

2. Copying, Cutting, and Pasting Text

The phone allows you to copy or cut text from one location and paste it to another. Copying leaves the text in its current location and allows you to paste it elsewhere. Cutting deletes the text from its current location and allows you to paste it elsewhere. To cut, copy, and paste text:

1. Touch and hold text on the screen. The Text options appear, as shown in **Figure 4**. To learn how to compose a message, refer to *"Composing a New Text Message"* on page 53.
2. Touch one of the following options to perform the associated action:

   - **SELECT ALL** (touch the ⠿ icon first) - Selects all of the text in the field.
   - **CUT** - Removes the text and copies it to the clipboard. Touch and hold any white field, even in an outside application, and touch **Paste** to enter the cut text.
   - **COPY** - Leaves the text in the field and copies it to the clipboard. Touch and hold any white field, even in an outside application, and touch **Paste** to enter the copied text.

Note: The 'cut' and 'copy' options only become available when text is selected.

Figure 4: Text Options

3. Using the Auto-Complete Feature

While typing a text message, the phone automatically makes suggestions to auto-complete words, which appear above the virtual keyboard, as outlined in **Figure 5**. This is especially useful when a word is very long. To accept a suggestion, touch the word. The word is inserted into the current message.

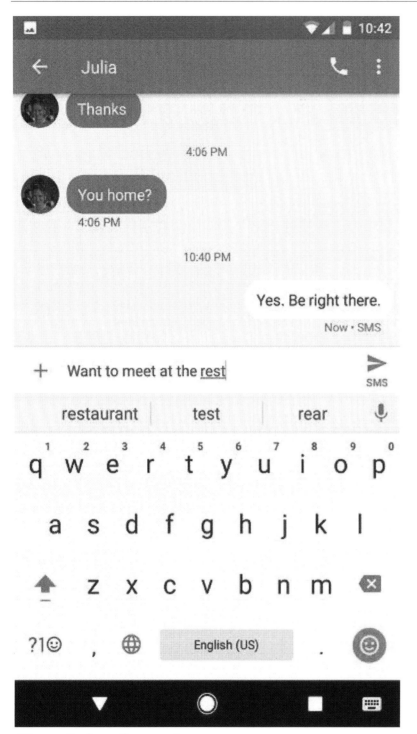

Figure 5: Auto Suggestions

4. Switching to an Alternate Language

While entering a text message, you can switch your keyboard to display a non-English keyboard. Before switching to another keyboard, you must add it via the Keyboard Settings screen. Refer to *"Changing the Input Method"* on page 286 to learn how. To switch to another language, touch the icon. The alternate keyboard appears.

5. Receiving Text Messages

The phone can receive text messages from any other mobile phone, including non-smartphones. When receiving a text, the phone vibrates twice, plays a sound, or both, depending on the settings. Refer to *"Changing the Ringtones"* on page 241 to learn how to set text message notifications.

If the screen is locked, the text message alert appears on the screen, as shown in **Figure 6**. Touch the text message twice to open the text conversation.

To open a newly received text message when the screen is unlocked, touch the text message at the top of the screen, as shown in **Figure 7**.

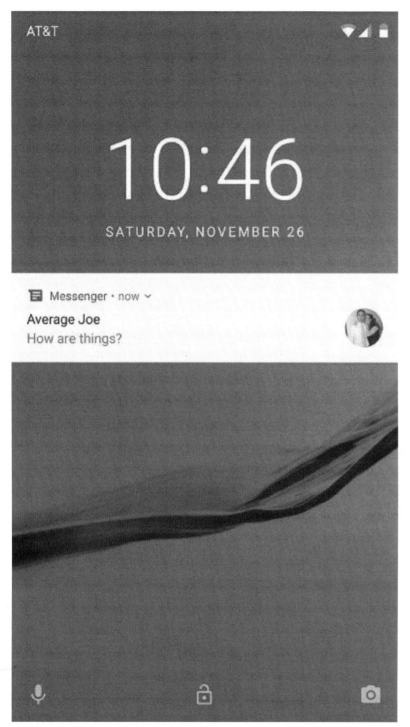

Figure 6: New Text Message on the Lock Screen

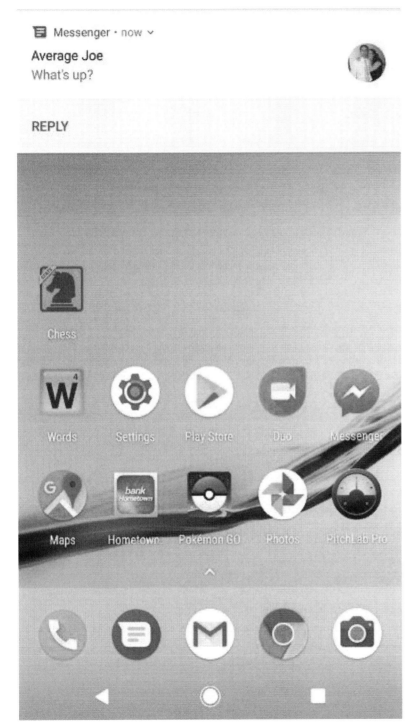

Figure 7: New Text Message on the Home Screen

6. Reading Text Messages

You may read any text messages that you have received, provided that you have not deleted them.

To read stored text messages, touch the ![icon] icon. The Messaging screen appears. Touch a conversation. The conversation opens.

7. Forwarding Text Messages

The forwarding feature allows a text message to be copied in full and sent to other recipients. To forward a text message:

1. Touch the ![icon] icon. The Messaging screen appears.
2. Touch a conversation. The Conversation opens.
3. Touch and hold a text message. The Message options appear, as outlined in **Figure 8**.
4. Touch the ![icon] icon at the top of the screen. The Forward Message window appears.
5. Touch the ![icon] icon. The New Message screen appears with a list of the most frequently contacted people.
6. Touch the name of a contact in the list, or enter a phone number. Suggestions appear while typing. The addressee or phone number is entered. A conversation with the selected contact is created, or an existing conversation appears, and the original message is pasted in the message field.
7. Touch the ![icon] button. The text message is forwarded.

Figure 8: Message Options

8. Calling the Sender from within a Text

After receiving a text message from a contact, you may call that person without exiting the text

message. To call someone while viewing a text conversation, touch the ![icon] icon at the top of the screen. The phone automatically dials the contact's number.

9. Viewing Sender Information from within a Text

You can look up a contact's details without exiting the Messaging application. To view the information of the person who sent you a text message, touch the letter next to the conversation between you and that contact, or touch the person's picture, if one is assigned. The Contact Information screen appears, as shown in **Figure 9**. Touch the top of the screen to hide the contact's information.

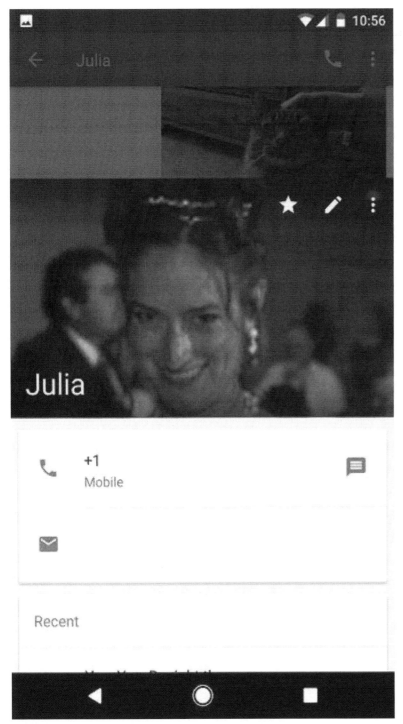

Figure 9: Contact Information Screen

10. Deleting Text Messages

You can delete separate text messages or an entire conversation, which is a series of text messages between you and one or more contacts.

Warning: Once deleted, text messages cannot be restored.

To delete an entire conversation:

1. Touch the  icon. The Messaging screen appears.

2. Touch and hold a conversation. The Conversation is selected and a 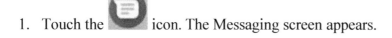 mark appears next to it, as shown in **Figure 10**. Touch any additional conversations that you would like to delete.

3. Touch the ![trash] icon at the top of the screen. A Confirmation dialog appears.
4. Touch **DELETE**. The conversation is deleted.

To delete a separate text message:

1. Touch the ![messaging] icon. The Messaging screen appears.
2. Touch a conversation. The conversation opens.
3. Touch and hold a text message. The Message options appear.

4. Touch the ![trash] icon at the top of the screen. The message is deleted.

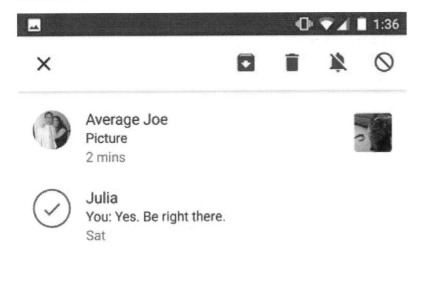

Figure 10: Selected Conversation

11. Adding Texted Phone Numbers to Contacts

A phone number contained in a text message may be immediately added to the phonebook as a new contact. To save a texted phone number as a contact:

1. Touch the ![icon] icon. The Messaging screen appears.
2. Touch a conversation. The conversation opens.
3. Touch the phone number in the text message. The keypad appears, with the phone number pasted in the number field. If you have another calling application installed, you may need to touch **Phone** before the keypad appears.
4. Touch **Add to a contact** at the top of the screen. The phonebook appears, as shown in **Figure 11**. You may touch a name in the list to add the phone number to an existing contact. Otherwise, touch **Create new contact**. The Add new contact screen appears, as shown in **Figure 12**.

5. Enter the name of the contact, and fill in any other fields, as necessary. Touch the ![icon] icon at the top of the screen. The new contact is saved to the phonebook.

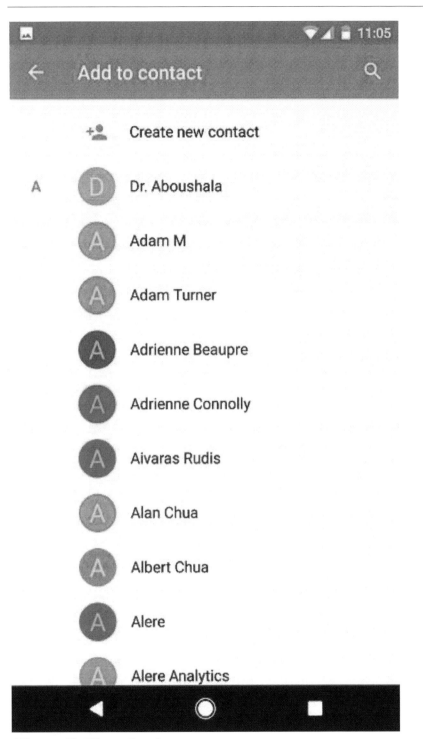

Figure 11: Phonebook

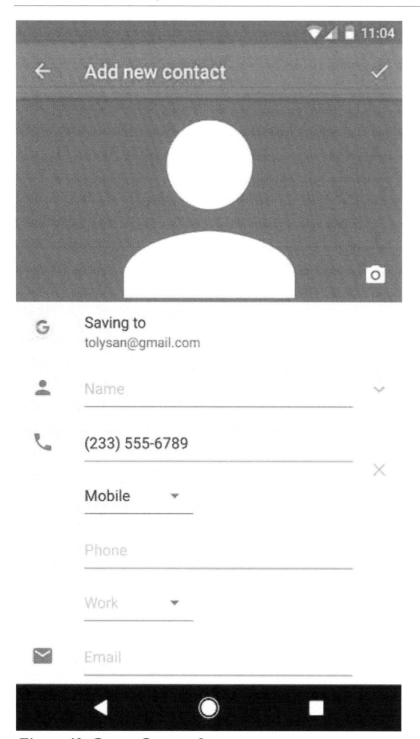

Figure 12: Create Contact Screen

12. Adding an Attachment to a Text Message

A picture, video, or other file can be attached to any text message. To send a text message with an attachment:

1. Refer to *"Composing a New Text Message"* on page 53 and follow steps 1-3.
2. Touch the ✦ icon to the left of the 'Type an SMS message' field. The camera turns on, as shown in **Figure 13**. If you previously attached a photo from the gallery or a voice recording, the corresponding screen appears in the lower half of the screen.
3. Refer to one of the following sections to learn how to attach the associated media:
   * *"Attaching a Picture"* on page 75
   * *"Attaching a Video"* on page 78
   * *"Attaching a Voice Recording"* on page 80
4. Touch an attachment to view it or touch the ⊗ icon to remove it.

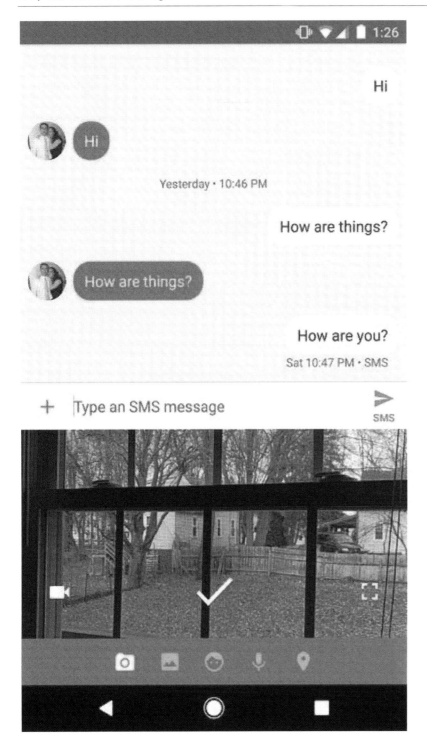

Figure 13: Camera On

13. Attaching a Picture

The phone can send media messages containing pictures. To attach a picture to a text message:

1. Refer to *"Adding an Attachment to a Text Message"* on page 73 and follow steps 1-2. The Attachment menu appears.
2. Follow the steps in the appropriate section below:

Taking and Attaching a Picture

Touch the 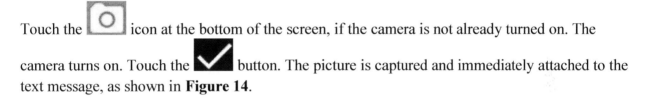 icon at the bottom of the screen, if the camera is not already turned on. The camera turns on. Touch the 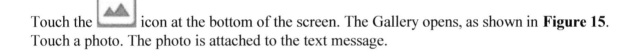 button. The picture is captured and immediately attached to the text message, as shown in **Figure 14**.

Attaching a Picture from a Photo Album

Touch the 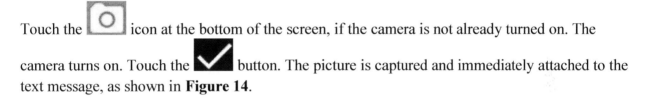 icon at the bottom of the screen. The Gallery opens, as shown in **Figure 15**. Touch a photo. The photo is attached to the text message.

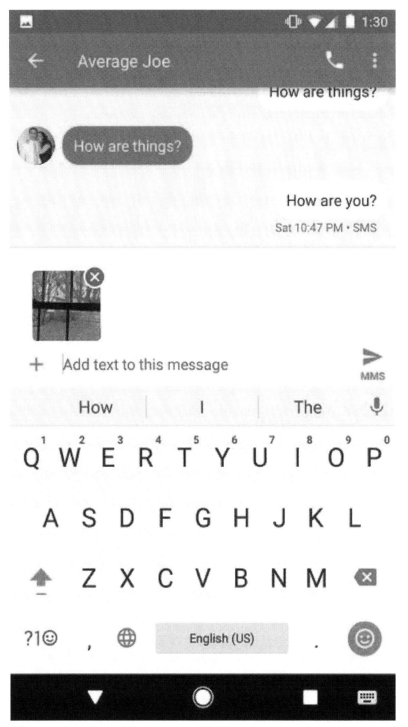

Figure 14: Text Message with Picture Attached

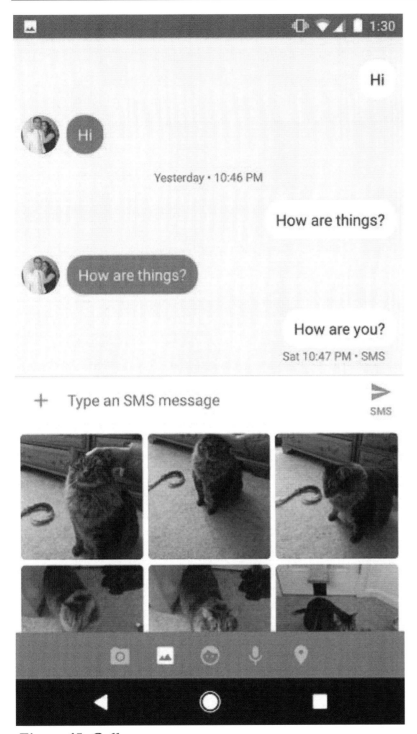

Figure 15: Gallery

14. Attaching a Video

The phone can send media messages containing videos. To attach a video to a text message:

1. Refer to *"Adding an Attachment to a Text Message"* on page 73 and follow steps 1-2. The Attachment menu appears.
2. Follow the steps in the appropriate section below:

Attaching a Video from the Camcorder

1. Touch the icon at the bottom of the screen, if the camera is not already turned on. The camera turns on.
2. Touch the button. The video begins to record.
3. Touch the button. The camcorder stops recording and the video is immediately attached to the text message, as shown in **Figure 16**. Touch the attached video once to preview it.

Note: The camcorder will automatically stop recording when the video has reached the maximum size limit.

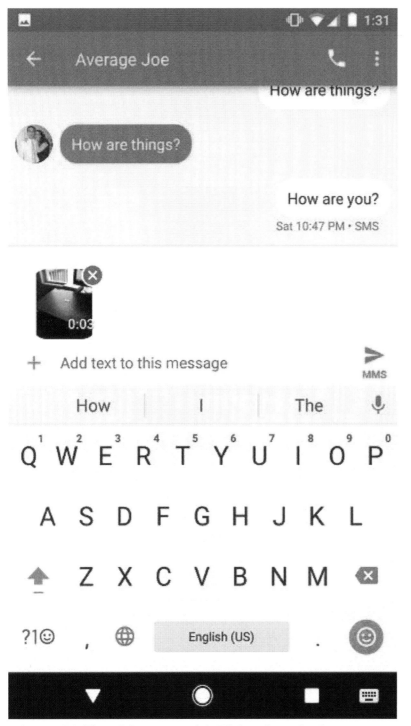

Figure 16: Text Message with Video Attached

15. Attaching a Voice Recording

The phone can send media messages containing voice recordings. To attach a voice recording to a text message:

1. Refer to *"Adding an Attachment to a Text Message"* on page 73 and follow steps 1-2. The Attachment menu appears.

2. Touch the 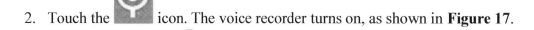 icon. The voice recorder turns on, as shown in **Figure 17**.

3. Touch and hold the  button. The phone starts recording.

4. Release the ![button] button. The recording is attached to the text message, as shown in **Figure 18**.

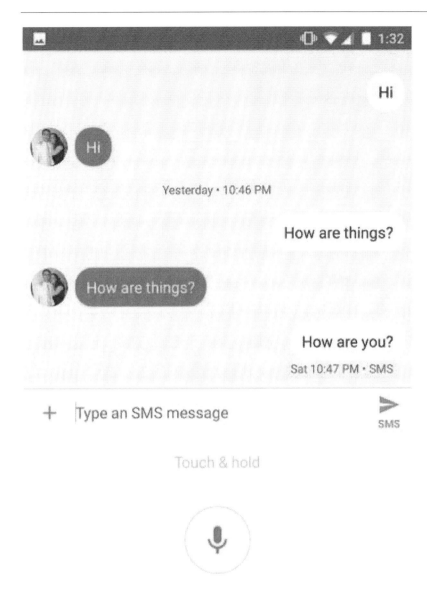

Figure 17: Voice Recorder

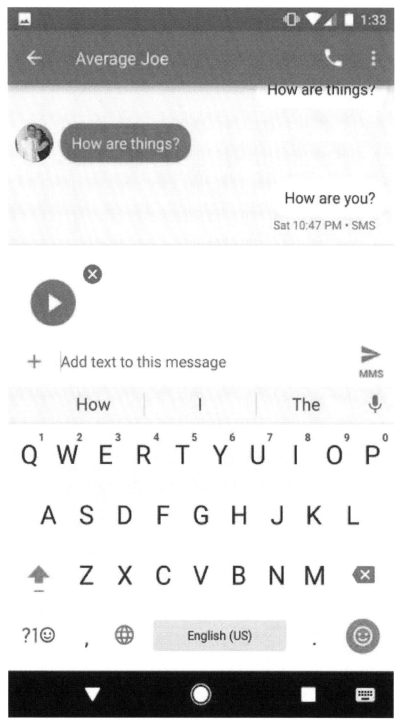

Figure 18: Text Message with Voice Recording Attached

16. Saving Attachments from Text Messages

After receiving an attachment in a text message, it can be saved to your phone. To save an attachment from a text message:

1. Touch the icon. The Messaging screen appears.
2. Touch a conversation. The conversation opens.
3. Touch and hold the attachment in the text message. The Attachment options appear, as outlined in **Figure 19**.

4. Touch the icon at the top of the screen. The attachment is saved to the phone.

Figure 19: Attachment Options

17. Archiving a Text Conversation

You may wish to remove a text conversation from the Messaging screen and save it to your phone for future reference. To archive a conversation, touch it and move your finger to the left or right until the conversation has disappeared. The conversation is archived.

To restore a conversation from the archive, touch the icon at the top of the screen, then

touch **Archived** to view the archive. Touch and hold a conversation, and then touch the icon. The conversation is now visible on the Messaging screen.

18. Turning Off Text Message Notifications for a Specific Contact

If someone is annoying you, you may want to temporarily stop receiving text message notifications from that person. To turn off notifications for a specific contact:

1. Touch and hold the conversation. The Conversation menu appears.

2. Touch the 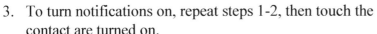 icon at the top of the screen. Notifications for the contact are turned off.

3. To turn notifications on, repeat steps 1-2, then touch the icon. Notifications for the contact are turned on.

19. Blocking a Contact

If you no longer wish to receive text messages or calls from a contact, you may block them

completely. To block a contact, touch and hold the conversation, then touch the icon. The contact is blocked and the conversation is archived.

If you wish to unblock a contact, touch the icon at the top of the screen, then touch **Blocked Contacts**. Touch the icon next to the contact that you want to unblock.

Managing Pixel Users

Table of Contents

1. Adding a User

The phone allows you to have multiple user profiles, each with different settings and applications. To add a user to the phone:

1. Touch the bottom of any Home screen, then slide up your finger. Touch the icon. The Settings screen appears, as shown in **Figure 1**. Refer to *"Tips and Tricks"* on page 296 to learn how to quickly access the Settings screen.
2. Touch **Users**. The Users Settings screen appears, as shown in **Figure 2**.
3. Touch **Add user**. A confirmation dialog appears.
4. Touch **OK**. Touch **Set Up Now** in the following dialogue. The Lock screen appears, and you can now set up the new user.
5. Unlock the screen by swiping up. The Welcome screen appears.
6. Touch **Continue**. The Google Account screen appears, as shown in **Figure 3**.
7. Enter your Google credential and touch **Next**, or touch **CREATE A NEW ACCOUNT**. Otherwise, touch **SKIP** to do this later.
8. Touch **Agree** to agree to the Terms of Service, then touch **All Set** on the following screen. The new user account is set up and ready to use.

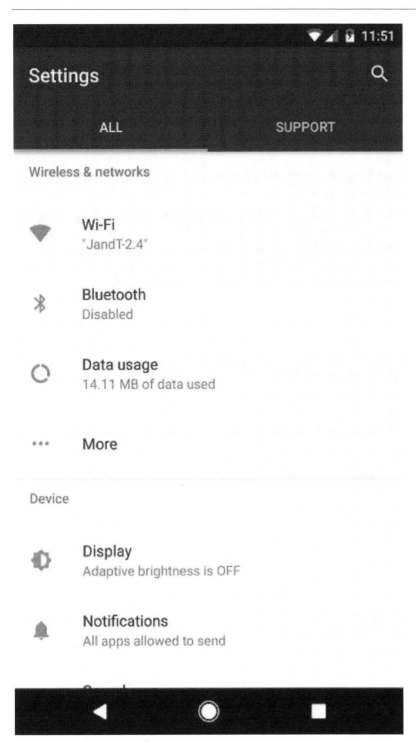

Figure 1: Settings Screen

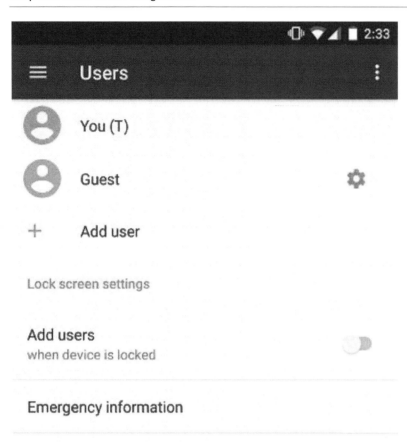

Figure 2: Users Settings Screen

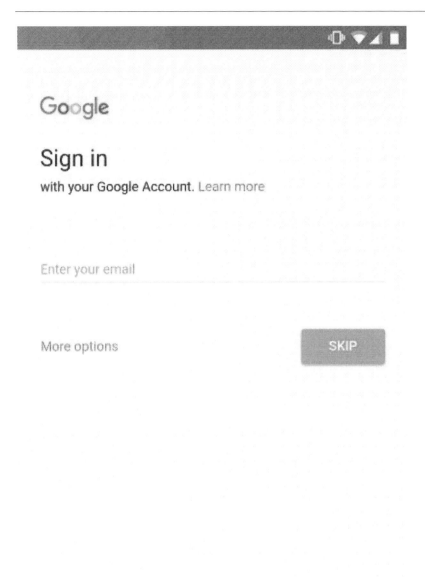

Figure 3: Google Account Screen

2. Deleting a User Profile

If a particular user no longer needs to use the phone, you may delete their profile. Only the original user of the phone can delete other user profiles. To delete a user profile:

Warning: Deleting a user profile permanently erases all of the user's settings and files that have not been uploaded to the Cloud.

1. Touch the bottom of any Home screen, then slide up your finger. Touch the icon. The Settings screen appears.
2. Touch **Users**. The Users Settings screen appears.

3. Touch the ⚙ icon next to a user's name. The User Information screen appears, as shown in **Figure 4**.
4. Touch **Remove user**. A confirmation dialog appears.
5. Touch **DELETE**. The user profile is deleted.

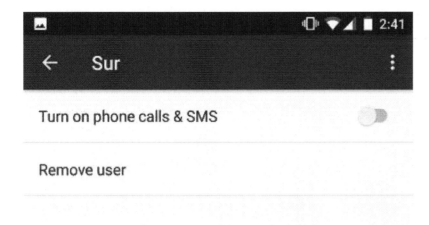

Turn on phone calls & SMS

Remove user

Figure 4: User Information Screen

3. Switching Users

You can switch between users at any time. To switch to a different user:

1. Touch the top of the screen when the phone is locked or unlocked, then slide your finger down. The Notifications screen appears. If the phone is unlocked, touch the top of the screen using two fingers and slide down.

2. Touch the icon. A list of available users appears, as shown in **Figure 5**.
3. Touch the name of the user. The phone switches to the selected user.

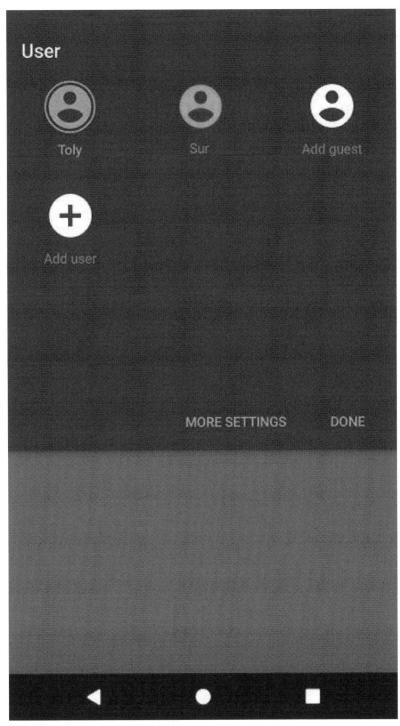

Figure 5: List of Available Users

4. Using the Phone as a Guest

If you do not want to create a separate user account, you can have someone use the phone as a guest. A guest receives a clean slate as if they just started using the phone. The guest does not have access to the main user's applications, contacts, or any other personal data. In addition, a guest's progress is saved, and the option to continue from where the guest last left off is given when logging back in as a guest. To use the phone as a guest:

1. Touch the top of the screen when the phone is locked or unlocked, and slide your finger down. The Notifications screen appears. If the phone is unlocked, you will need to slide your finger down twice.

2. Touch the icon. A list of available users appears.

3. Touch **Add guest**. The Guest account is ready to use.

If you have used the Guest account on the phone in the past, touch **Guest**. A Welcome Back window appears. Touch **YES, CONTINUE** to retain your applications and settings from the last time that you used the account. Otherwise, touch **START OVER**.

Note: You can clear the guest user's data from the phone by touching the *icon and then touching* **Remove guest**.

5. Using Application Pinning for Children

The Pixel lets you pin, or lock, a single application, which prevents the user from leaving that application. This is especially useful for allowing your children to use the phone without worrying about their surfing the web or checking your email. To use application pinning:

1. Touch the bottom of any Home screen, then slide up your finger. Touch the   icon. The Settings screen appears.
2. Touch **Security**. The Security Settings screen appears, as shown in **Figure 6**.
3. Touch **Screen Pinning**. The Screen Pinning screen appears, as shown in **Figure 7**.
4. Touch **Off**. The feature is turned on.
5. Open the application that you want to pin. Then, touch the ▢ key. A list of all recent applications appears.
6. Touch the screen and move your finger up. The ▢ icon becomes visible, as shown in **Figure 8**.
7. Touch the ▢ icon. The application is pinned. To exit the pinned application, touch and hold the ◀ key.

You can also lock the device using a passcode in case your child accidentally unpins the screen. To do so, touch **Lock device when unpinning** on the Screen Pinning screen.

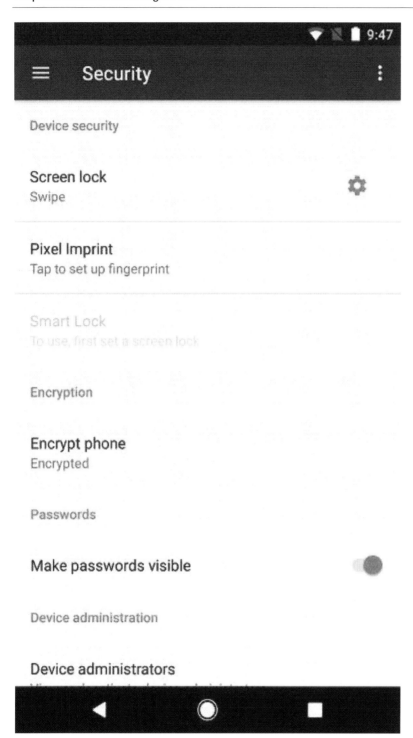

Figure 6: Security Settings

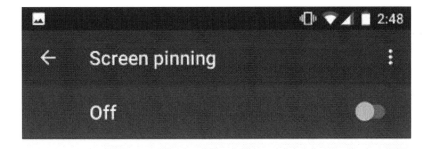

When this setting is turned on, you can use screen pinning to keep the current screen in view until you unpin.

To use screen pinning:

1. Make sure screen pinning is turned on.

2. Open the screen you want to pin.

3. Tap Overview.

4. Swipe up and then tap the pin icon.

Figure 7: Screen Pinning Screen

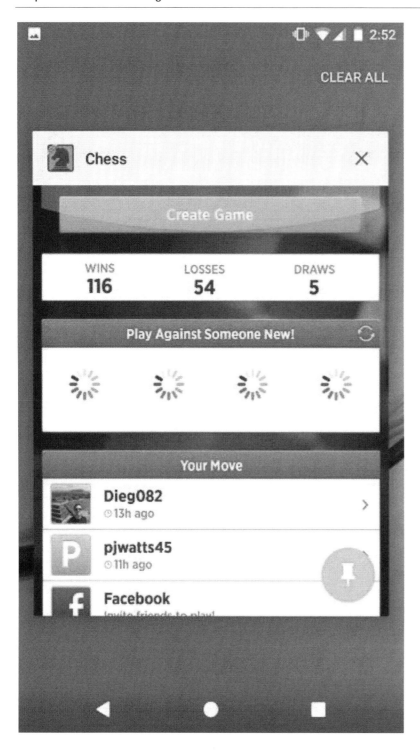

Figure 8: Screen Pinning Icon

Managing Applications

Table of Contents

Refer to *"Tips and Tricks"* on page 296 to learn about performing quick application actions right from the Home screen.

1. Setting Up a Google Account

In order to buy applications, you will need to assign a Google account to the phone. Refer to *"Setting Up the Gmail Application"* on page 155 to learn how to assign a Google account to the phone.

2. Searching for Applications

There are two ways to search for applications: perform a manual search or browse by category.

Manual Search

To search for an application manually:

1. Touch the bottom of any Home screen and slide your finger up, then touch the 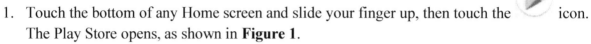 icon. The Play Store opens, as shown in **Figure 1**.
2. Touch **Google Play** at the top of the screen. The keyboard appears.
3. Enter the name of an application and touch the key. All matching results appear, as shown in **Figure 2**.
4. Touch the name of an application. A description of the application appears. Refer to *"Purchasing Applications"* on page 105 to learn how to buy the selected application.

Browse by Category

View applications by genre, such as games, travel, or productivity. To browse applications by category:

1. Touch the bottom of any Home screen and slide your finger up, then touch the icon. The Play Store opens.
2. Touch **Categories**. A list of application categories appears, as shown in **Figure 3**.
3. Touch a category. The category screen appears, as shown in **Figure 4**. You can touch **Top Charts** to view the most popular applications in the category.
4. Touch the name of an application. A description of the application appears. Refer to *"Purchasing Applications"* on page 105 to learn how to buy the selected application.

Note: Some applications, such as games, may have sub-categories (i.e. racing, puzzle, arcade). For these cases, repeat steps 2 and 3 to browse the sub-categories.

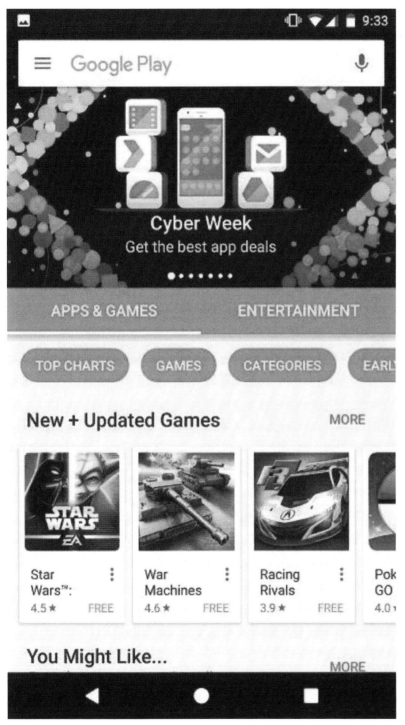

Figure 1: Play Store

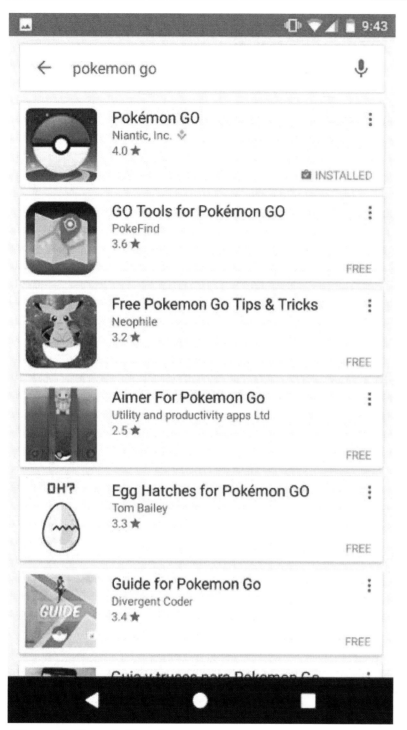

Figure 2: Search Results

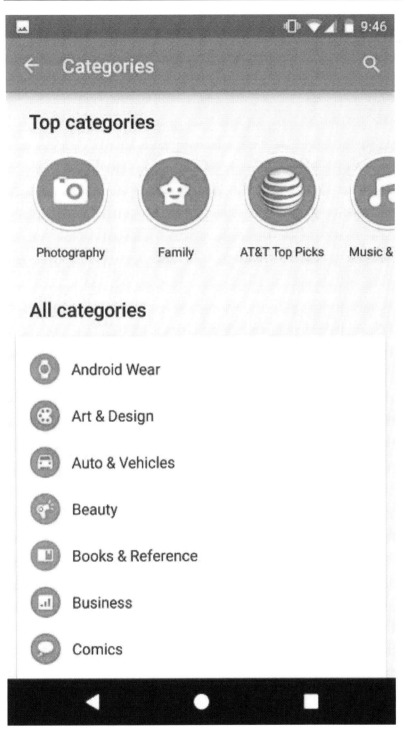

Figure 3: List of Application Categories

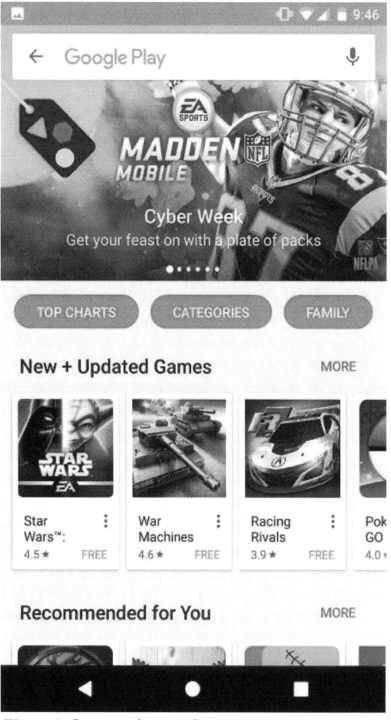

Figure 4: Category Screen (Games)

3. Purchasing Applications

Applications can be purchased directly from the phone using the Play Store. To buy an application:

1. Touch the bottom of any Home screen and slide your finger up, then touch the 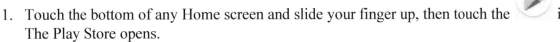 icon. The Play Store opens.
2. Find the application that you wish to purchase. Refer to *"Searching for Applications"* on page 100 to learn how.
3. Touch the name of an application. The Application Description screen appears, as shown in **Figure 5** (free application) and **Figure 6** (paid application).
4. Follow the appropriate instructions below to download the application:

Installing Free Applications

Touch **INSTALL**. The application is downloaded and installed. The download progress is shown on the Application Description screen while the application is downloading. Touch **OPEN** to open the downloaded application. The application opens.

Refer to *"Types of Home Screen Objects"* on page 15 and *"Organizing Home Screen Objects"* on page 17 to learn more about accessing applications.

Installing Paid Applications

1. Touch the price of the application. The Purchase screen appears, as shown in **Figure 7**. If you have not provided your credit card information, Google Checkout will request the information when you purchase an application for the first time. The information is saved and the Purchase Confirmation screen appears.
2. Touch **BUY**. If this is the first time that you are purchasing an application, the Password Confirmation dialog appears.
3. Enter your password and touch **OK**. The application is purchased, downloaded, and installed. The download progress is shown on the Application Description screen while the application is downloading.
4. Touch **OPEN** to open the purchased application. The application opens. Refer to *"Types of Home Screen Objects"* on page 15 and *"Organizing Home Screen Objects"* on page 17 to learn more about accessing applications.

 War Machines Tank Shooter Game

Fun Games For Free

Everyone 10+

INSTALL

Contains ads • In-app purchases

 1 MILLION Downloads   4.6 66,542   Action   Similar

It's war! Join now explosive multiplayer tank battles

Free Tank Shooting Game

READ MORE

Figure 5: Application Description Screen (Free Application)

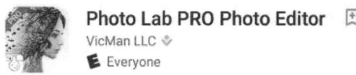

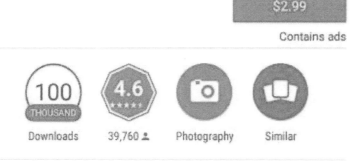

READ MORE

Figure 6: Application Description Screen (Paid Application)

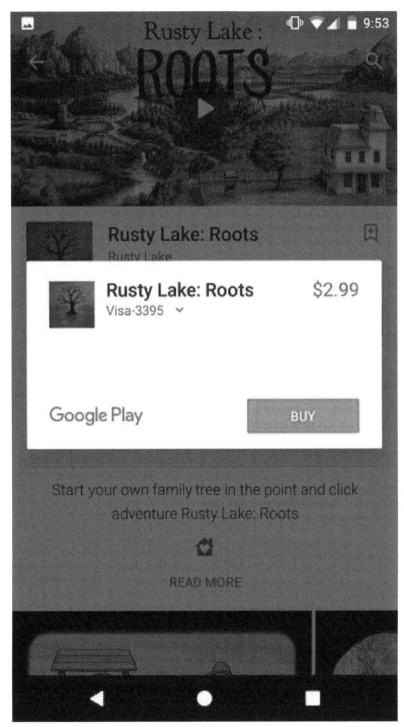

Figure 7: Purchase Screen

4. Uninstalling an Application

Within the first 15 minutes of purchasing an application, it can be uninstalled for a full refund. After 15 minutes have passed, the following instructions only apply to uninstalling an application with no refund. An application that you have purchased can always be re-downloaded for free, unless you touch **REFUND**, in which case you need to purchase the application again. To uninstall an application:

1. Touch the bottom of any Home screen and slide your finger up, then touch the icon. The Play Store opens.
2. Touch the left-hand side of the screen, then slide your finger to the right. The Play Store menu appears, as shown in **Figure 8**.
3. Touch **My apps & games**. The My apps screen appears, as shown in **Figure 9**.
4. Touch an application. The Installed Application Description screen appears, as shown in **Figure 10**.
5. Touch **REFUND** if less than 15 minutes have passed since the application was purchased. Otherwise, touch **Uninstall**. A confirmation dialog appears.
6. Touch **YES**. The application is uninstalled and a full refund is given if you touched **REFUND**.

Note: Refer to "Quickly Uninstalling Applications" *on page 298 to learn how to uninstall an application without opening the Play Store.*

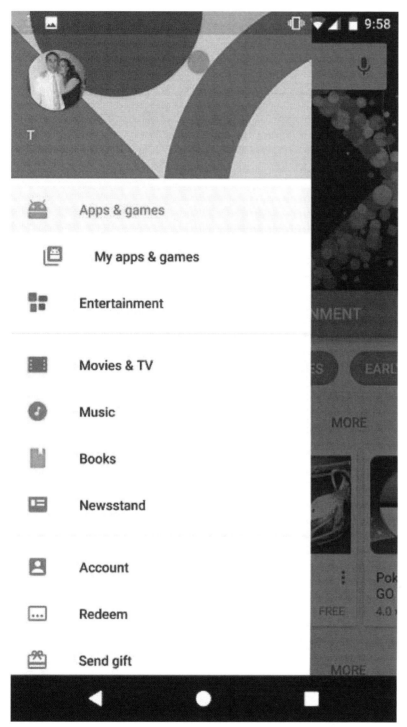

Figure 8: Play Store Menu

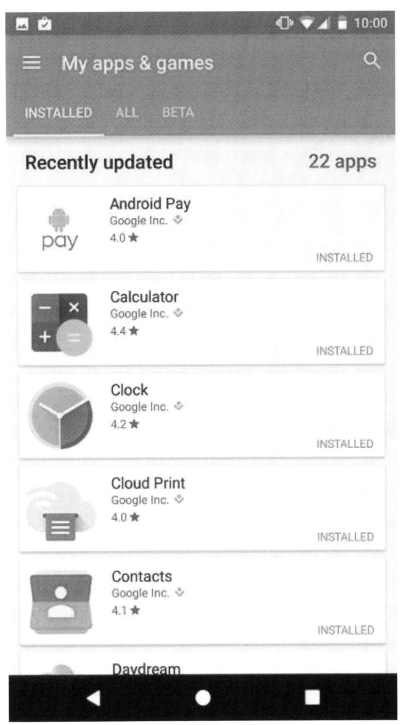

Figure 9: My Apps Screen

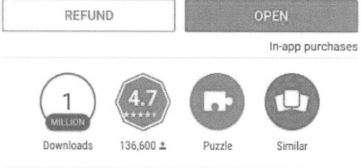

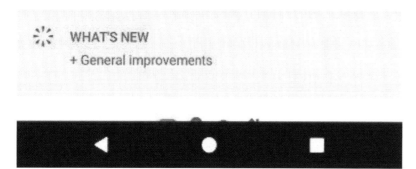

Figure 10: Installed Application Description Screen

5. Sharing an Application Link via Email

The phone allows you to share applications with friends via email. When sharing an application, a link to the application's page in the Play Store is sent. Those with whom links are shared will still need to pay for the shared applications that they purchase. To share an application via email:

1. Touch the bottom of any Home screen and slide your finger up, then touch the 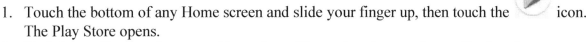 icon. The Play Store opens.
2. Find the application that you wish to share. If you already own the application that you wish to share, touch the left side of the screen in the Play Store, and then touch **My apps & games** to browse your installed applications. Otherwise, refer to *"Searching for Applications"* on page 100 to learn how to find an application for sale in the Play Store.
3. Touch the name of an application. The Application Description screen appears.
4. Scroll down and touch the icon. A list of Sharing options appears.
5. Touch the icon in the list of Sharing options. A new email is composed with a link to the shared application pasted into the message, as shown in **Figure 11**.
6. Enter the recipient's email address. The email address is entered.
7. Touch the button. The email is sent.

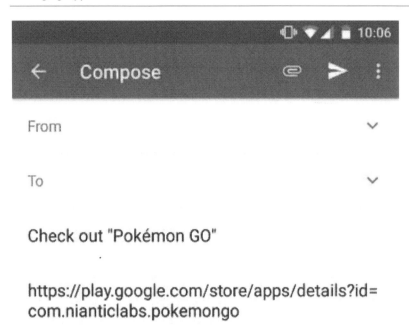

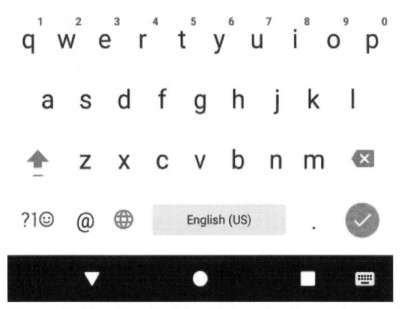

Figure 11: New Email with a Link to the Shared Application

6. Viewing Recently Opened Applications

Most applications will keep running in the background even after they are exited, and some require a considerable amount of memory and battery life. To view the recent applications, touch

the ▢ key at any time. The Overview screen appears, as shown in **Figure 12**. Overview creates multiple cards for a single application, if necessary. For example, when you compose a new email, both your inbox and the new email appear in Overview, and you can switch freely between the two. When using a Web browser, separate tabs appears in separate windows in Overview, unless your settings indicate otherwise.

Closing Open Applications

To speed up the performance of the phone and conserve battery life, try closing some or all of these applications while they are not in use. To close an application running in the background, touch and hold an application in Overview, then drag it to the left or right. The application is closed.

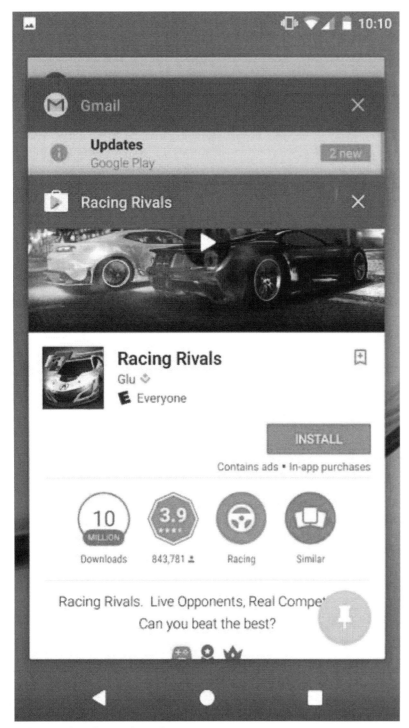

Figure 12: Overview Screen

7. Reading User Reviews

Reading user reviews may help when making a decision between similar applications from different developers. Unlike certain websites, the Play Store does not allow those who have not downloaded an application to review it. However, be advised that fake reviews are often posted either to boost ratings or tarnish the reputation of the developer. To read user reviews for an application:

1. Touch the bottom of any Home screen and slide your finger up, then touch the   icon. The Play Store opens.
2. Find an application. Refer to *"Searching for Applications"* on page 100 to learn how.
3. Touch the name of the application. The Application Description screen appears.
4. Touch the screen and move your finger up to scroll to the bottom of the page. The reviews for the current application are found below the application screenshots, as shown in **Figure 13**.

3.9 ★★★✫☆
843,781 ☺

REVIEW HIGHLIGHTS

best racing game   in 959 reviews

"It is really fun to pass the time and the best racing game their is keep up the good work"

addictive   in 640 reviews

"...Graphics improved and more. It's addicting again. Thanks for fixing the game again GLU..."

good graphics   in 596 reviews

"...This game has really good graphics, cars, and events. And it looks and feels realistic..."

fast cars   in 473 reviews

"This is the best , most realistic drag racing game . Awesome graphics and fast cars..."

many bugs   in 101 reviews

"With the new update there are too many bugs and the graphics look worse"

Figure 13: User Reviews

8. Managing Payment Methods

Add a credit card to your Google account to purchase applications or other media from the Play Store. To manage your payment methods:

1. Touch the bottom of any Home screen and slide your finger up, then touch the icon. The Play Store opens.
2. Touch the left-hand side of the screen, then slide your finger to the right. The Play Store menu appears.
3. Touch **Account**. The Account screen appears, as shown in **Figure 14**.
4. Touch **Payment method**s. The Payment Methods screen appears, as shown in **Figure 15**.
5. Touch the icon. The Add payment method screen appears, as shown in **Figure 16**.
6. Touch the type of payment that you want to use. Enter the credit card or other information on the following screens. If using PayPal, you will only need to enter the email address and password associated with your account.

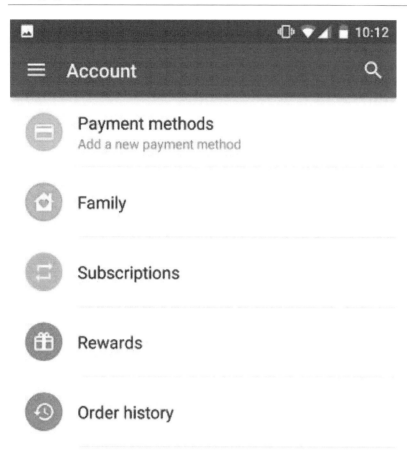

Figure 14: Account Screen

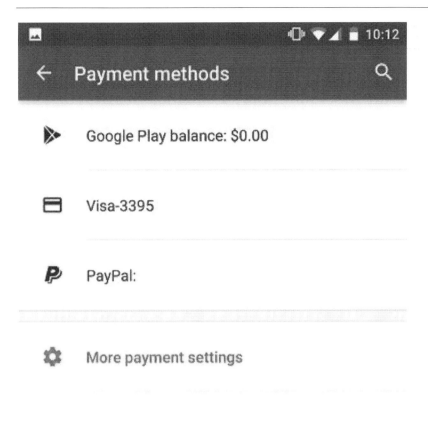

Figure 15: Payment Methods Screen

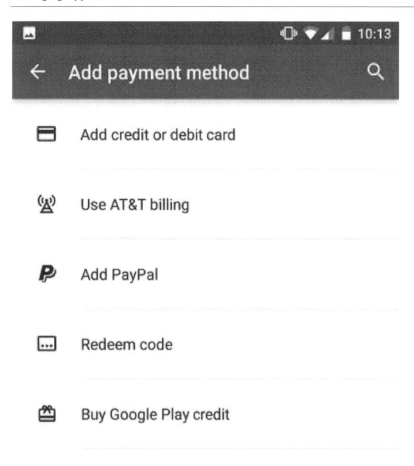

Figure 16: Add Payment Method Screen

9. Redeeming a Play Store Gift Card

When you receive a Play Store gift card, you must redeem it before using it to purchase media in the Play Store. Redeeming a gift card adds the balance on the card to your Play Store account. When you have used the entire balance, your regular payment method is used to purchase media. To redeem a Play Store gift card:

1. Touch the bottom of any Home screen and slide your finger up, then touch the icon. The Play Store opens.
2. Touch the left-hand side of the screen, and slide your finger to the right. The Play Store menu appears.
3. Touch **Redeem**. The Code Redemption screen appears, as shown in **Figure 17**.
4. Enter the code on your Play Store gift card. You may need to scratch the code on the card to reveal it, as indicated on the card.
5. Touch **Redeem**. The gift card is redeemed, and the card balance is added to your Play Store balance.

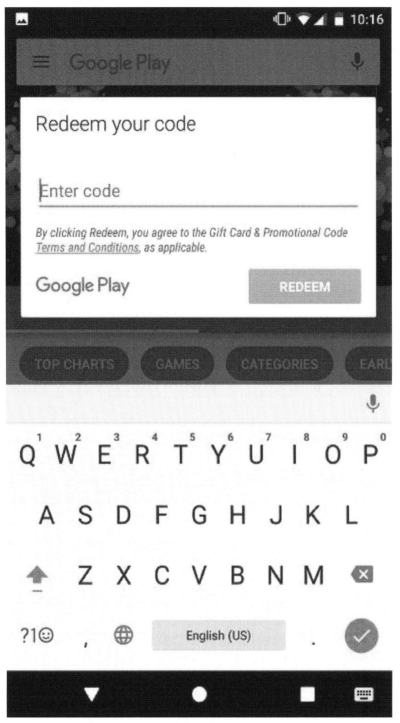

Figure 17: Code Redemption Screen

Taking Pictures and Capturing Videos

Table of Contents

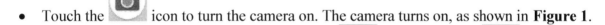

1. Taking a Picture

The Pixel has a 12.3-megapixel rear-facing and an 8-megapixel front-facing camera. To take a picture:

- Touch the ⬛ icon to turn the camera on. The camera turns on, as shown in **Figure 1**.

- To switch to the front-facing camera, touch the ⬛ icon. Touch the ⬛ icon again to switch to the rear-facing camera.

- Touch the ⬛ button to take a picture. A picture is captured and stored in the photo library.

Note: Refer to "Browsing Pictures" *on page 138 to learn how to browse the pictures in your Gallery.*

Figure 1: Camera Turned On

2. Using the Digital Zoom

While taking pictures or capturing videos, use the Digital Zoom feature if the subject of the photo is far away. To zoom in, touch the screen with two fingers and move them apart. To zoom out, touch the screen with two fingers spread apart and move them together.

Note: Because of its digital nature, the zoom function will not provide the best resolution, and the image may look fuzzy. It is recommended to be as close as possible to the subject of the photo or video.

3. Turning the Photo Location On or Off

The phone can store the location where a photo was captured. However, you may choose to turn this feature off. To turn the photo location feature on or off while the camera is turned on:

1. Touch the left side of the screen, and slide your finger to the right. The Camera Menu appears, as shown in **Figure 2**.
2. Touch **Settings**. The Camera Settings screen appears, as shown in **Figure 3**.
3. Touch **Save location**. The ⬤ switch appears and Photo Location is turned off.
4. Touch **Save location** again. The ⬤ switch appears and Photo Location is turned on.

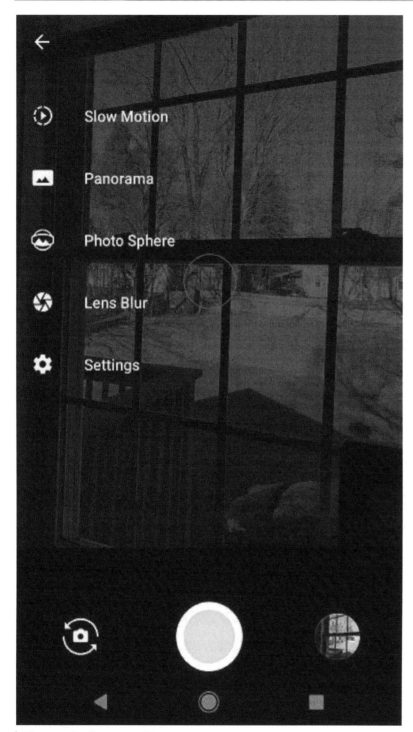

Figure 2: Camera Menu

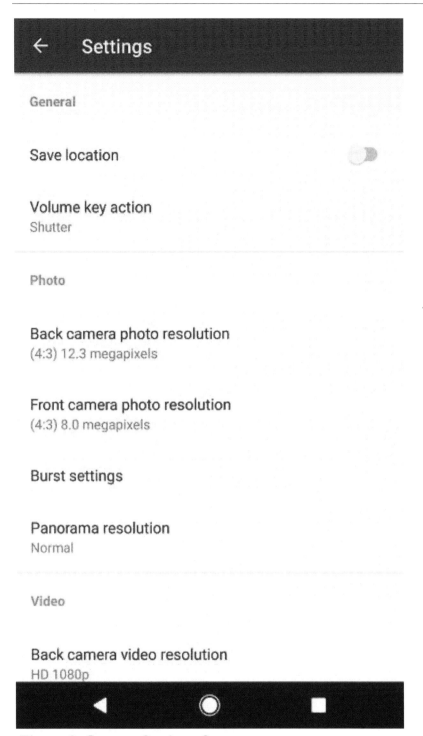

Figure 3: Camera Settings Screen

4. Turning the Countdown Timer On or Off

If you would like to capture a picture of several people, including yourself, you may wish to set a

timer. To turn the countdown timer on or off when the camera is turned on, touch the ![timer icon] icon,
then touch **3 seconds**, **10 seconds**, or **Timer off**.

5. Setting the Picture or Video Size

You may set the resolution of a photo or video before you take it. A higher resolution will produce
a higher quality photo or video, but will take up more memory. To set the resolution of a picture:

1. Touch the left side of the screen, and slide your finger to the right. The Camera Menu
   appears.
2. Touch **Settings**. The Camera Settings screen appears.
3. Touch one of the following options to set the corresponding resolution:
   - **Back camera photo resolution** - Set the resolution for photos captured using the
     rear-facing camera
   - **Front camera photo resolution** - Set the resolution for photos captured using the
     front-facing camera
   - **Back camera video resolution** - Set the resolution for videos captured using the
     rear-facing camera
   - **Front camera video resolution** - Set the resolution for videos captured using the
     front-facing camera
4. Touch the ![back key] key to return to the camera. The resolution settings are saved until the
   next time that you change them, or until you reset the phone to factory defaults.

6. Adjusting the Exposure

You may adjust the amount of light that is allowed to enter the camera lens, a concept known as
the exposure. This will make a picture lighter or darker, depending on the setting. To adjust the

exposure, touch anywhere on the screen, then touch the ![exposure icon] icon, as outlined in **Figure 4**. Slide
your finger up or down to increase or decrease the exposure, respectively.

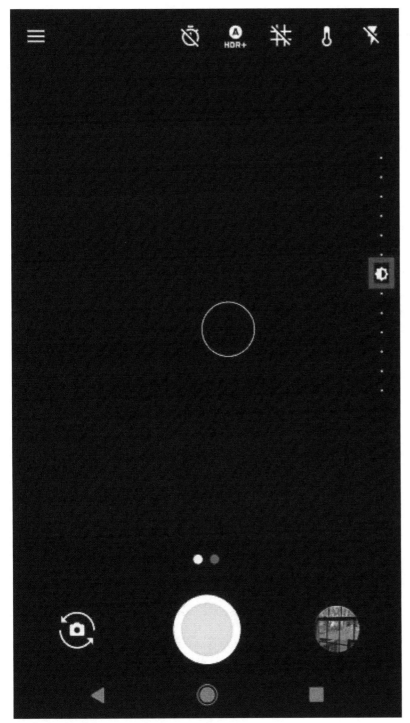

Figure 4: Exposure Icon Outlined

7. Creating a Panorama

The camera on the phone allows you to take a 360-degree panoramic photo by capturing several images and automatically patching them together. To take a panorama while the camera is turned on:

1. Touch the left side of the screen, and slide your finger to the right. The Camera Menu appears.
2. Touch **Panorama**. The Panorama instructions appear only when you use this feature for the first time.
3. Touch **GOT IT**. The camera is ready to capture a 360-degree panorama, as shown in **Figure 5**.
4. Align the circle in the middle of the screen with the first frame of your panorama, and touch the button at the bottom of the screen. The camera captures the first image. There is no need to touch any buttons.
5. Move the phone in any direction and align the circle in the middle of the screen with the next dot. Try to stay in one place and simply rotate with the phone. The camera captures another image. Repeat step 4 until you have captured all of the space around you. The spherical panorama is rendered and stored in your photo library.

You can also capture a spherical panorama using a similar process. To do so, touch **Photo Sphere** in the Camera Menu, then follow steps 4-5 above.

Figure 5: Camera Ready to Capture a 360-Degree Panorama

8. Capturing a Video

The camcorder on the phone allows you to capture video. To capture a video:

1. Touch the icon. The camera turns on.
2. Touch anywhere on the screen and slide your finger to the left. The camcorder turns on.
3. Touch the button at the bottom of the screen. The camcorder begins to record video, as shown in **Figure 6**.
4. Touch the button. The camcorder stops recording, and the video is stored in the photo library.

Figure 6: Camcorder Recording a Video

9. Turning the Flash On or Off

The Pixel has a built-in LED flash, which can be used when taking a picture or capturing a video using the rear-facing camera. To use the flash when taking a picture or capturing a video:

1. Touch the icon at the top of the screen. The Flash options appear, as shown in **Figure 7**.
2. Touch one of the following icons to turn the flash on or off:

   - The flash is set to Automatic mode. When Automatic mode is turned on, the light sensor on the rear-facing camera determines whether the flash is needed.

   - The flash is turned off.

   - The flash is turned on permanently.

Note: Automatic mode is not available when capturing a video.

Figure 7: Flash Options

Managing Photos and Videos

Table of Contents

1. Browsing Pictures

You can browse captured or saved photos using the Gallery application. To view the images stored on your phone:

1. Touch the icon on the Home screen, or touch the bottom of any Home screen and slide up your finger, then touch the icon. The Gallery opens, as shown in **Figure 1**. By default, the photos are sorted by date.

2. To browse the photos by album, touch **Albums** at the bottom of the screen. The Photo Albums appear, as shown in **Figure 2**. Touch an album to open it.

3. Touch a photo. The image appears in Full-Screen mode. Touch the key to return to the photo thumbnails.

Tuesday

Monday

Sunday

Friday, Nov 25

Figure 1: Gallery

Figure 2: Photo Albums

2. Starting a Slideshow

The phone can play slideshows using the pictures stored in the Gallery. To start a slideshow:

1. Touch a photo thumbnail. The photo opens in full screen.
2. Touch the ⋮ icon in the upper right-hand corner of the screen. The Photo options appear, as shown in **Figure 3**.
3. Touch **Slideshow**. The slideshow begins.
4. Touch the screen once. The slideshow stops.

Figure 3: Photo Options

3. Applying Special Effects to Pictures

Pictures stored on the phone can be cropped, rotated, and enhanced with various effects. To edit a picture:

1. Open a photo. The image appears in full-screen mode. Refer to *"Browsing Pictures"* on page 138 to learn how to open an image.

2. Touch the [icon] at the bottom of the screen. The Photo is opened for editing, as shown in **Figure 4**.

3. Follow the steps in the appropriate section below to learn how to use the various editing options:

Adjusting the Lighting and Color Settings

There are several options that allow you to adjust the amount of light and color in an image. To adjust the lighting and color settings:

1. Follow the instructions above. Then, touch the [icon] at the bottom of the screen. The Image Tuning screen appears, as shown in **Figure 5**.

2. You can make the following adjustments to the photo:
   - **Light** - Adjust the amount of light in the photo.
   - **Color** - Adjust the intensity of the colors in the photo.
   - **Pop** - Adjust the different in the amount of light and color between different parts of the photo. Higher pop results in a sharper photo. This is also known as contrast.

3. Touch **Save**. The change is applied to the photo and a copy of the original is saved with your adjustments.

Applying Color Effects

There are several color effects that may be applied to a photo. To add a color effect,

follow the instructions at the beginning of this section, then touch the [icon] icon at the bottom of the screen. The Color Effects menu appears, as shown in **Figure 4**. Touch an effect in the list, then touch Save. The change is applied to the photo and a copy of the original is saved with your adjustments.

Figure 4: Photo Editing Menu

Figure 5: Image Tuning Screen

4. Cropping a Picture

You may crop a photo to use a specific piece of it. To crop a photo:

1. Open a photo. Refer to *"Browsing Pictures"* on page 138 to learn how to open an image.
2. Touch the ✏️ at the bottom of the screen. The Photo is opened for editing.
3. Touch the 🔳 icon at the bottom of the screen. The cropping markers appear on the photo, as shown in **Figure 6**.
4. Touch the corners of the photo, then drag them to resize the crop. The crop is resized.
5. Touch inside the white rectangle, and drag it around to select the portion of the photo that you would like to use. The portion of the photo is selected.
6. Touch **Done**. The cropped photo is saved.
7. Touch **Save**. The change is applied to the photo and a copy of the original is saved with your adjustments.

Figure 6: Cropping Markers on a Photo

5. Flipping or Rotating a Picture

You may rotate a photo in 90 degree increments, or flip it to view it upside down or as a mirror image. To flip or rotate a picture:

1. Open a photo. Refer to *"Browsing Pictures"* on page 138 to learn how to open an image.
2. Touch the 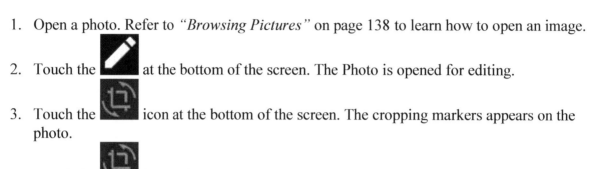 at the bottom of the screen. The Photo is opened for editing.
3. Touch the icon at the bottom of the screen. The cropping markers appears on the photo.
4. Touch the icon. The photo is rotated 90 degrees counterclockwise. You can also touch the rotation adjustment bar to rotate manually.
5. Touch **Done**. The rotated photo is saved.
6. Touch **Save**. The change is applied to the photo and a copy of the original is saved with your adjustments.

6. Deleting Pictures

Warning: Once a picture is deleted, there is no way to restore it.

To free up some space in the phone's memory, try deleting some pictures from the Gallery. To delete a picture:

1. Open a photo album. Refer to *"Browsing Pictures"* on page 138 to learn how to open a photo album.
2. Touch and hold a photo. The photo is selected, and a check mark appears on the thumbnail, as outlined in **Figure 7**. Touch all other photos that you wish to delete.
3. Touch the 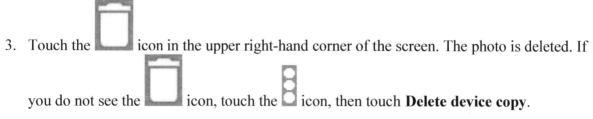 icon in the upper right-hand corner of the screen. The photo is deleted. If you do not see the icon, touch the icon, then touch **Delete device copy**.

Camera

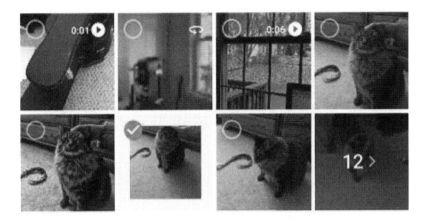

Screenshots

Figure 7: Selected Photo

7. Importing and Exporting Pictures Using a PC or Mac

Pictures and other files can be transferred to and from the phone. Refer to *"Exporting and Importing Files Using a PC or Mac"* on page 19 to learn how.

8. Sharing a Photo or Video via Email

You may share media by attaching it to an email. This method of transferring photos to your own computer takes much longer than the one discussed in *"Exporting and Importing Files Using a PC or Mac"* on page 19 because the images can be somewhat large in size when taken on the phone. To share a photo or video:

1. Open a photo album. Refer to *"Browsing Pictures"* on page 138 to learn how.
2. Touch and hold a photo. The photo is selected, and a check mark appears on the thumbnail. Touch any other photos that you wish to share.

3. Touch the ![share icon] icon, then touch the ![M icon] icon. A new email appears with the selected photos attached, as shown in **Figure 8**.

4. Touch the ![send button] button. The email with the attached photos is sent.

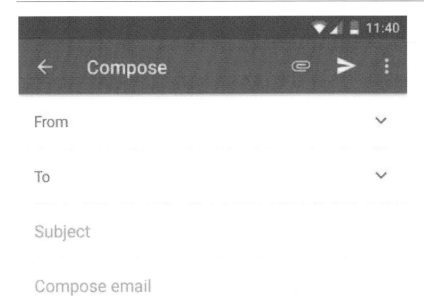

Figure 8: Photos Attached to an Email

9. Creating a Movie Using a Photo Collection

You can create an enhanced slideshow, or movie, using the pictures in your photo library. To create a movie:

1. Touch the ![icon] icon on the Home screen, or touch the bottom of any Home screen and slide up your finger, then touch the ![icon] icon.
2. Touch **Assistant** at the bottom of the screen. The Assistant screen appears, as shown in **Figure 9**.
3. Touch **Movie**. The Photo Selection screen appears, as shown in **Figure 10**.
4. Touch **Select Items**. The photo thumbnails appear.
5. Touch the photos that you would like to use in your movie. Then, touch **Create**. The selected photos are used to create your movie. The movie is stored in the Movies album.

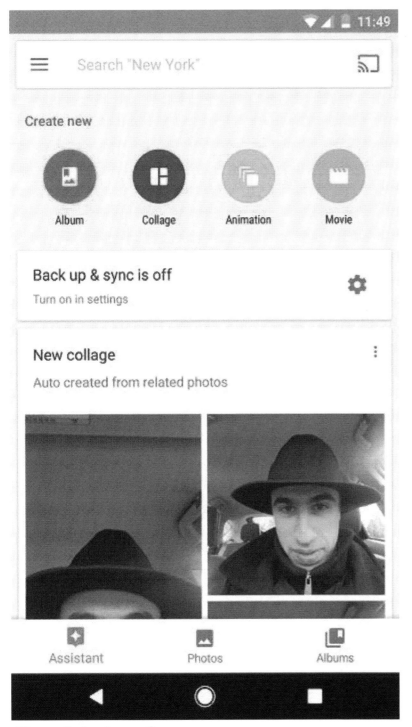

Figure 9: Assistant Screen

Select up to 50 photos or videos

Tuesday

Monday

Sunday

Friday, Nov 25

Figure 10: Photo Selection Screen

Using the Gmail Application

Table of Contents

1. Setting Up the Gmail Application

Before using the Gmail application, register a Google account to the phone. To add your Google account to the phone:

1. Touch the bottom of any Home screen, then slide up your finger. Touch the icon. The Settings screen appears, as shown in **Figure 1**.
2. Scroll down and touch **Accounts**. The Accounts screen appears, as shown in **Figure 2**.
3. Touch **Add account**. The Add an Account screen appears, as shown in **Figure 3**.
4. Touch **Google**, or touch **Exchange** or **Personal**, if you do not have a Google (Gmail) account. The Google Account screen appears, if you touched **Google**, as shown in **Figure 4**. The remaining instructions in this section apply only to Google accounts. For other accounts, follow the on-screen instructions, which usually consist of simply entering your email address and password.
5. Touch **Enter your email** if you already have a Google account. Otherwise, touch **More Options**, then touch **Create account** to create a new Google account. Once the account is created, it will be added to the phone automatically, and you may skip the rest of the steps in this section. If you would like to create your Google account using the Web browser on your computer, navigate to **https://accounts.google.com/SignUp** to do so.
6. Enter your Gmail address, and then touch **Next**. The password screen appears.
7. Enter your password, and touch **Next**. The Terms Agreement screen appears.
8. Touch **Agree**. The Google account is added to your phone.

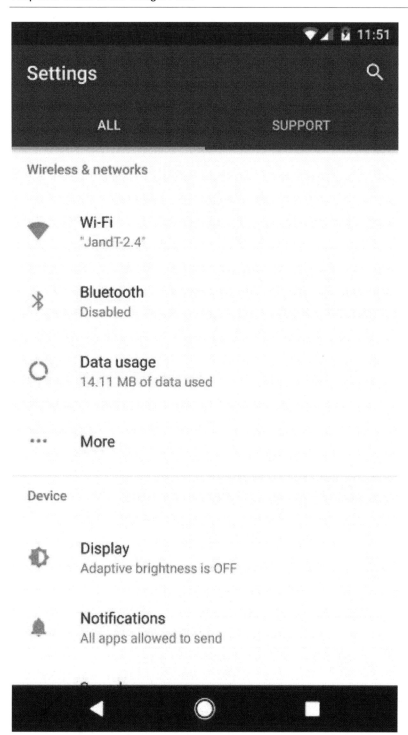

Figure 1: Settings Screen

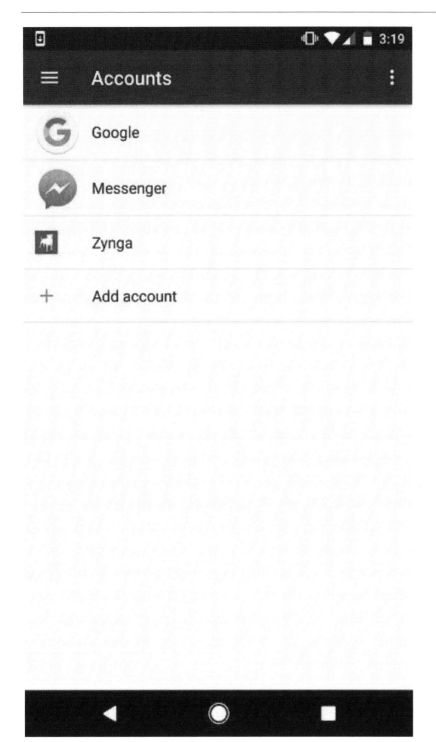

Figure 2: Accounts Screen

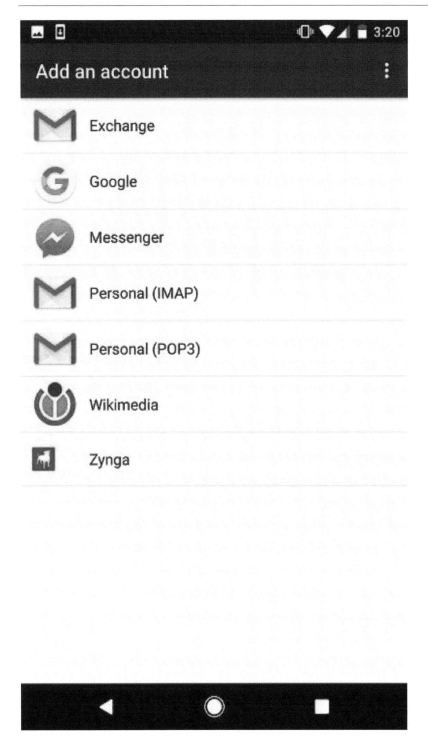

Figure 3: Add an Account Screen

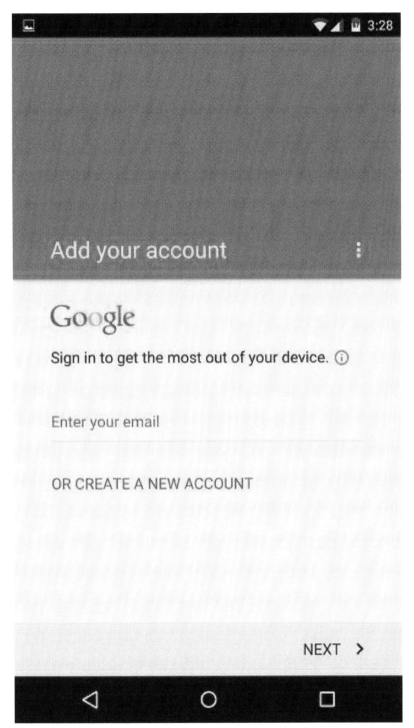

Figure 4: Google Account Screen

2. Reading Email

Since the phone is completely synced with every Google product, it is highly recommended to use a Gmail account on the phone. To read email using your Gmail account:

1. Touch the ![M] icon on the Home screen or touch the bottom of any Home screen, slide up your finger, and touch the ![M] icon. The Gmail application opens and the Inbox appears, as shown in **Figure 5**.
2. Touch an email. The email opens.
3. Touch the screen and move your finger to the left or right to view the previous or next email, respectively (where "previous" refers to an older email and "next" refers to a newer one).
4. To switch to a different account at any time, touch the left side of the screen, and slide your finger to the right. The Inbox menu appears, as shown in **Figure 6**.
5. Touch your email address at the top of the screen. The email addresses associated with Gmail accounts currently registered to the phone appear.
6. Touch an account name. The mailboxes associated with the account appear.

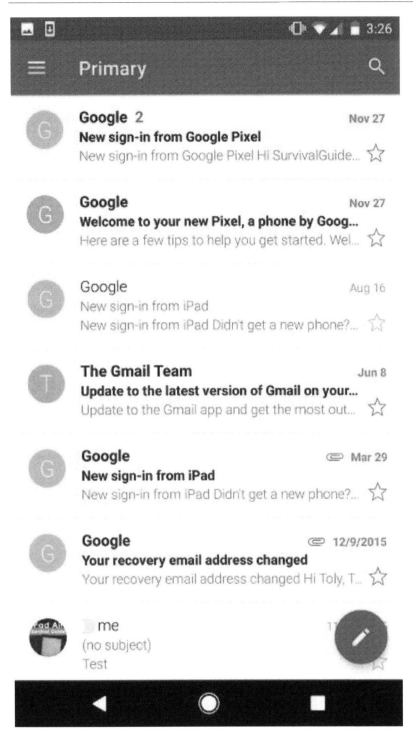

Figure 5: Gmail Inbox

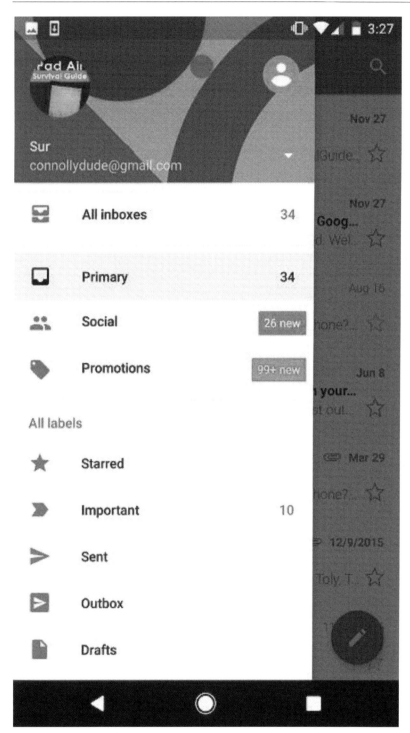

Figure 6: Inbox Menu

3. Writing an Email

Compose email directly from the phone using the Gmail application. To write an email:

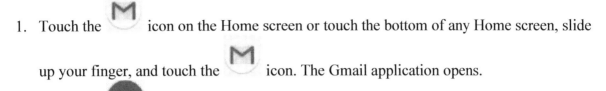

1. Touch the ⓜ icon on the Home screen or touch the bottom of any Home screen, slide up your finger, and touch the ⓜ icon. The Gmail application opens.

2. Touch the ✎ icon at the bottom of the screen. The Compose screen appears, as shown in **Figure 7**.

3. Start typing a name or email address. If the email address is stored in contacts, recipient suggestions appear while typing, as shown in **Figure 8**.

4. Touch **Subject** and enter the topic of the email. Touch **Compose email** and type the message. The message is entered.

5. Touch the ➤ button in the upper right-hand corner of the screen. The email is sent.

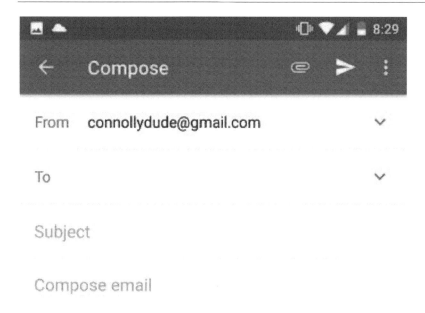

Figure 7: Compose Screen

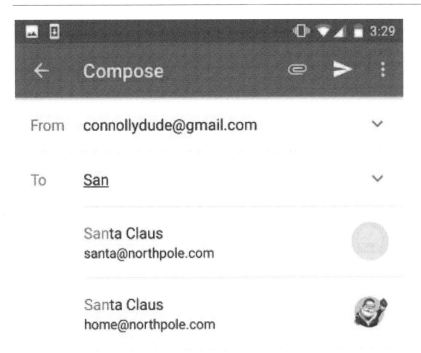

Figure 8: Recipient Suggestions

4. Replying to and Forwarding Emails

After receiving an email in the Gmail application, a direct reply can be sent, or the email can be forwarded. To reply to or forward an email:

1. Touch the icon on the Home screen or touch the bottom of any Home screen, slide up your finger, and touch the icon. The Gmail application opens.
2. Touch an email. The email opens.
3. Scroll down to the bottom of the email. Touch one of the following icons to perform the associated action, as outlined in **Figure 9**:

 - Send a reply to the sender.

- Send a reply to all recipients of the original email.

- Forward the email to a third party.

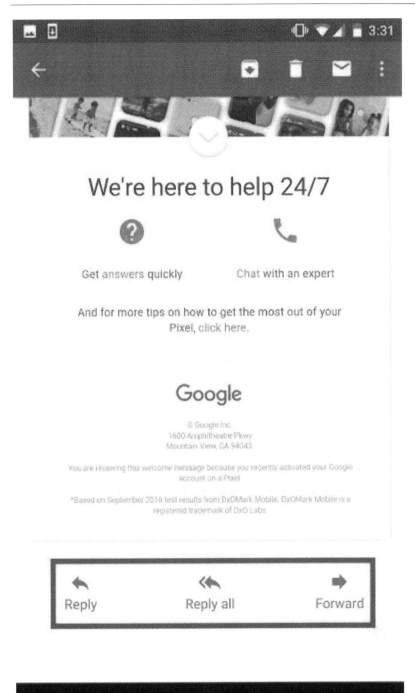

Figure 9: Email Options Outlined

5. Deleting and Archiving Emails

Deleting an email sends it to the Trash folder. To completely delete an email, the Trash folder must then be emptied using a Web browser (not covered in this guide). Otherwise, email will be automatically deleted from the Trash folder after 30 days. To delete an email:

1. Touch the ⓜ icon on the Home screen or touch the bottom of any Home screen, slide up your finger, and touch the ⓜ icon. The Gmail application opens.
2. Touch the letter or picture to the left of the email that you wish to delete. The letter is always the first letter of the name or service involved in the email conversation. For instance, if it is an email conversation with George, touch the Ⓖ icon. A picture appears next to an email if the contact is associated with your Google+ account. The email conversation is selected, and a check mark appears next to it. Touch the letter to the left of each email that you wish to delete, as shown in **Figure 10**.
3. Touch the 🗑 icon at the top of the screen. The selected email is deleted.

To clean up the Inbox without deleting emails, try archiving them. Archiving an email removes it from the Inbox and places it in the All Mail folder. Archived emails do not take up any space in your email inbox. To archive an email, touch the email in the Inbox and slide your finger to the left or right. 'Archived' appears in place of the email in the Inbox. Touch **undo** to return the email to the Inbox.

*Note: To find an archived email, touch the left side of the screen, then slide your finger to the right. Touch **All Mail**.*

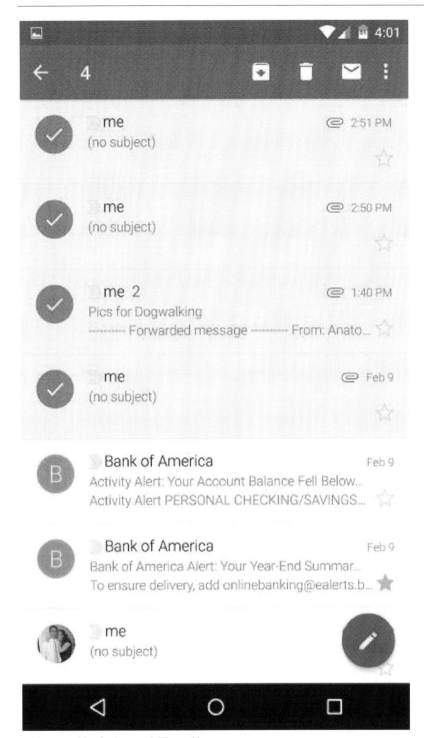

Figure 10: Selected Emails

6. Applying Labels to Emails

Emails can be classified according to the nature of the message, such as 'Work' or 'Personal'. Adding labels can help you to organize your inbox to find an email more quickly. To add a label to an email:

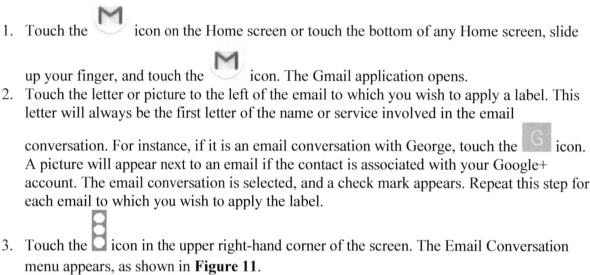

1. Touch the icon on the Home screen or touch the bottom of any Home screen, slide up your finger, and touch the icon. The Gmail application opens.
2. Touch the letter or picture to the left of the email to which you wish to apply a label. This letter will always be the first letter of the name or service involved in the email conversation. For instance, if it is an email conversation with George, touch the icon. A picture will appear next to an email if the contact is associated with your Google+ account. The email conversation is selected, and a check mark appears. Repeat this step for each email to which you wish to apply the label.
3. Touch the icon in the upper right-hand corner of the screen. The Email Conversation menu appears, as shown in **Figure 11**.
4. Touch **Change Labels**. A list of available labels appears, as shown in **Figure 12**.
5. Touch the labels in the menu that you wish to apply to the selected emails. A mark appears next to each selected label.
6. Touch **OK**. The selected labels are applied to the highlighted emails.

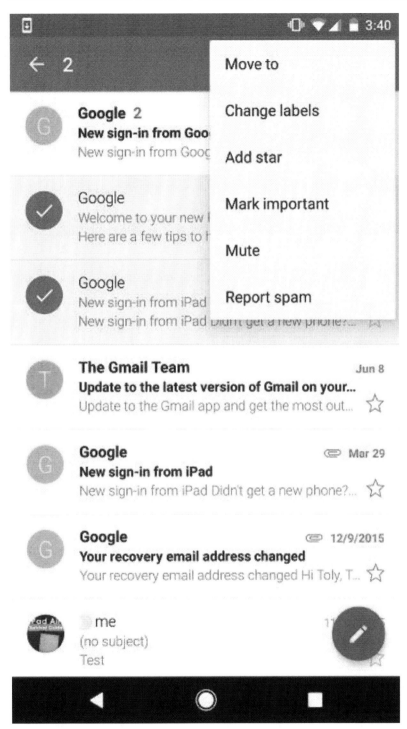

Figure 11: Email Conversation Menu

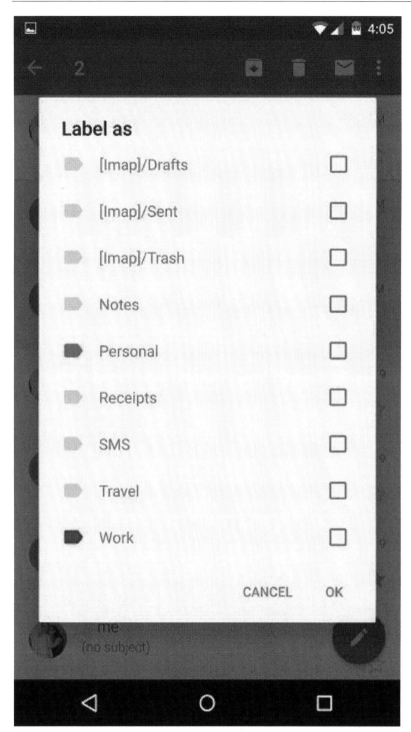

Figure 12: List of Available Labels

7. Searching the Inbox

To find a specific email in the Inbox, use the Search function, which searches email addresses, message text, and subject lines. To search the Inbox:

1. Touch the ![M] icon on the Home screen or touch the bottom of any Home screen, slide up your finger, and touch the ![M] icon. The Gmail application opens.
2. Touch the 🔍 icon at the top of the screen. The Search field appears at the top of the screen.
3. Enter a search term and touch the 🔍 key. The phone searches the Inbox and the matching results appear. Touch one of the results to open the email.

8. Adjusting the Gmail Settings

The Gmail application has several adjustable settings, such as the default signature, notification tones, and text size. To change these settings:

1. Touch the ![M] icon on the Home screen or touch the bottom of any Home screen, slide up your finger, and touch the ![M] icon. The Gmail application opens.
2. Touch the icon in the upper right-hand corner of the screen. The Inbox menu appears.
3. Scroll down and touch **Settings**. The Gmail Settings screen appears, as shown in **Figure 13**.
4. Touch **General settings**. The General Settings screen appears, as shown in **Figure 14**.
5. Touch one of the following options to perform the corresponding function:
   - **Conversation view** - Groups emails for email threads sent between a group of contacts.
   - **Sender image** - Shows the image assigned to the email sender.
   - **Reply all** - Uses the Reply All function as the default when you touch the icon.

- **Auto-advance** - Choose which screen the Gmail application shows after deleting or archiving an email.
- **Open web links in Gmail** - Enables faster browsing by opening links in emails within the Gmail application.
- **Confirm before deleting** - Display confirmations before deleting emails.
- **Confirm before archiving** - Display confirmations before archiving emails.
- **Confirm before sending** - Display confirmations when sending emails.
- **Clear Search History** (touch the ⦂ icon in the upper right-hand corner to access) - Clear the email search history to preserve privacy.
- **Clear picture approvals** (touch the ⦂ icon in the upper right-hand corner to access) - Pictures embedded in emails won't display automatically unless you allow them.

From the Gmail Settings screen, touch your email address, and then touch one of the following options to perform the corresponding action:

- **Inbox type** - Set whether the Default Inbox or the Priority Inbox is the default. The Priority Inbox will only display priority emails.
- **Inbox categories** - Set the categories that appear in the Inbox, such as 'Social' and 'Updates'. Google automatically sorts your email into these categories and displays them in separate Inboxes.
- **Notifications** - Turn on new Email notifications. The ✉ icon appears in the upper left-hand corner of the screen when a new email arrives. A ✓ mark next to 'Notifications' signifies that the feature is on.
- **Inbox sound & vibrate** - Display the Manage Labels screen, where you can choose which mailboxes display new email notifications and select the sound that plays when a new email arrives. You can also customize vibrations (smartphones only) on this screen. Touch **Sound** on the Manage Labels screen to select the Notification ringtone.
- **Signature** - Enter a default signature that will be attached to the end of each sent email.
- **Sync Gmail** - Turn automatic email retrieval on or off. A ✓ mark next to 'Sync Gmail' signifies that the feature is turned on.
- **Days of mail to sync** - Choose how many days in the past the Inbox should sync. For instance, if you select '3', the Gmail application will go back three days each time it syncs the email.
- **Manage Labels** - Brings you to the same screen as 'Ringtone & vibrate'.
- **Download attachments** - Turn on to have Gmail automatically download any attached files. A ✓ mark next to 'Sync Gmail' signifies that the feature is on.

Figure 13: Gmail Settings Screen

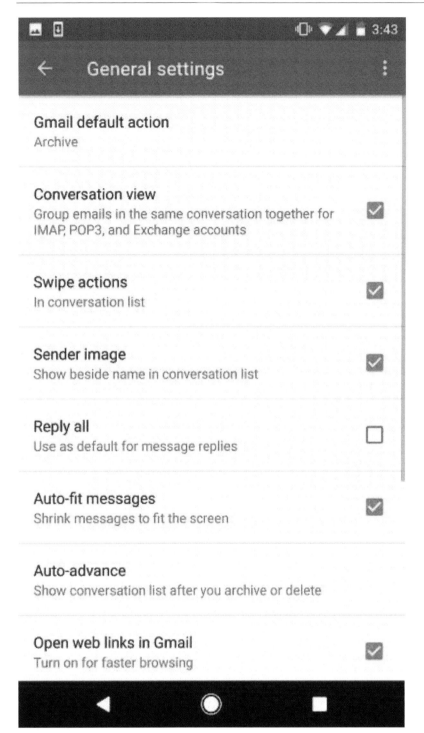

Figure 14: General Settings Screen

Managing Contacts

Table of Contents

1. Adding a New Contact

A contact can be added to the phonebook in your linked Google account. Adding a contact to a Google account allows total syncing of contacts across your phone and your online account. To add a new contact:

1. Touch the ![icon] icon on the Home screen or touch the bottom of any Home screen, slide up your finger, and touch the ![icon] icon. The Phonebook appears, as shown in **Figure 1**.

2. Touch the ![plus icon] icon. The New Contact screen appears, as shown in **Figure 2**.

3. Enter all desired information by touching each field to enter text. Touch the ![checkmark icon] icon at the top of the screen. The contact is stored in the phonebook.

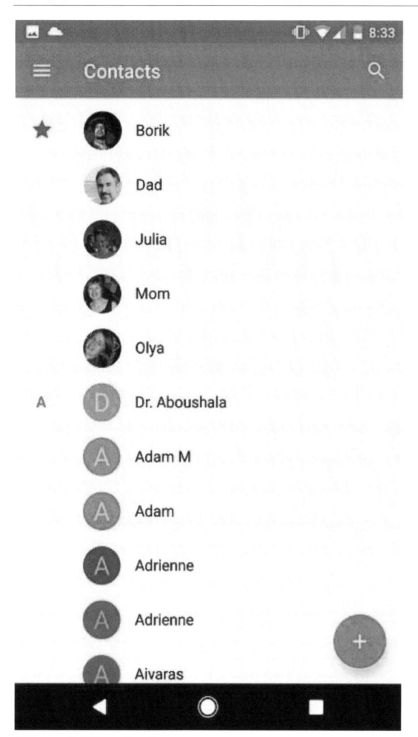

Figure 1: Phonebook

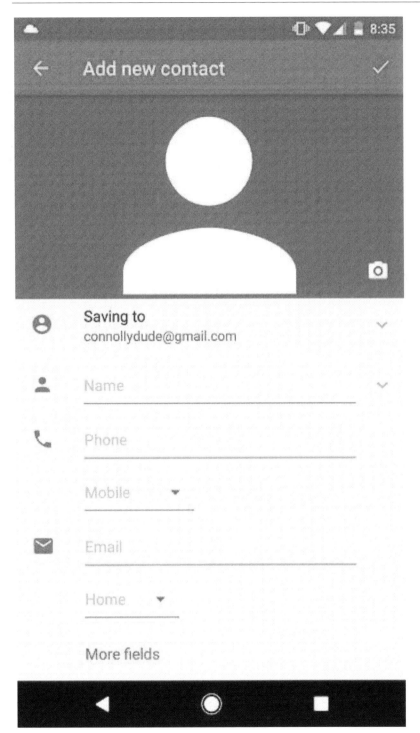

Figure 2: New Contact Screen

2. Creating a Shortcut to a Contact

The fastest way to consistently find a stored contact is to add a shortcut to the contact right from the Home screen. To create a shortcut to a contact:

1. Touch the icon on the Home screen or touch the bottom of any Home screen, slide up your finger, and touch the icon. The Phonebook appears.

2. Touch the name of the contact that you wish to add to the Home screen. The contact's information appears.

3. Touch the icon in the upper right-hand corner of the screen. The Contact menu appears, as outlined in **Figure 3**.

4. Touch **Place on Home screen**. A shortcut to the contact's information is added to the first available Home screen. The Contact shortcut may look similar to the icon in **Figure 4** if there is a picture assigned to the contact. If there is no picture assigned, the first letter of the contact's name is shown. Refer to *"Organizing Home Screen Objects"* on page 17 to learn how to move the new shortcut to another location or to place it in a folder.

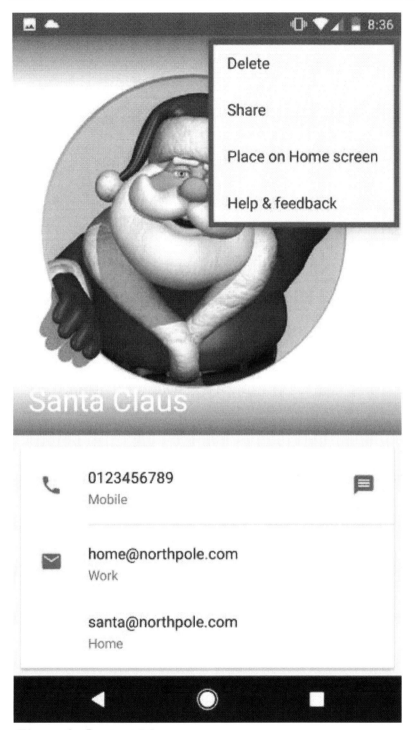

Figure 3: Contact Menu

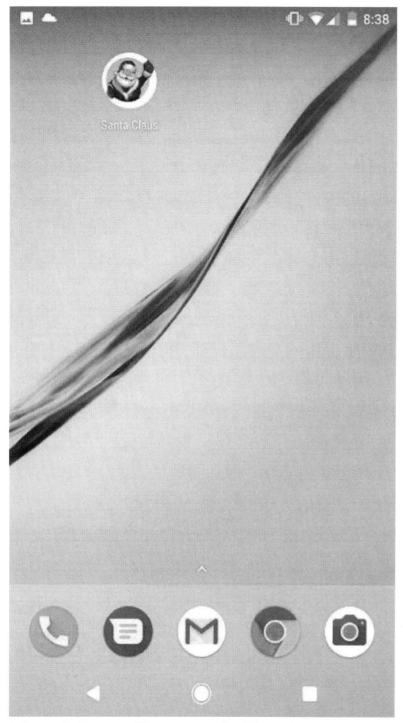

Figure 4: Contact Shortcut on the Home Screen

3. Editing Contact Information

Edit a contact entry to add additional information or to remove information that is no longer applicable, such as an email address or alternate phone number. To edit existing contact information:

1. Touch the icon on the Home screen or touch the bottom of any Home screen, slide up your finger, and touch the icon. The Phonebook appears.
2. Touch the name of the contact that you wish to edit. The contact's information appears.
3. Touch the icon at the top of the screen. The Edit Contact screen appears, as shown in **Figure 5**.
4. Touch a field to edit it. The field is selected.
5. Enter the new information, then touch the icon at the top of the screen when you are finished editing. The new information is stored in the phonebook.

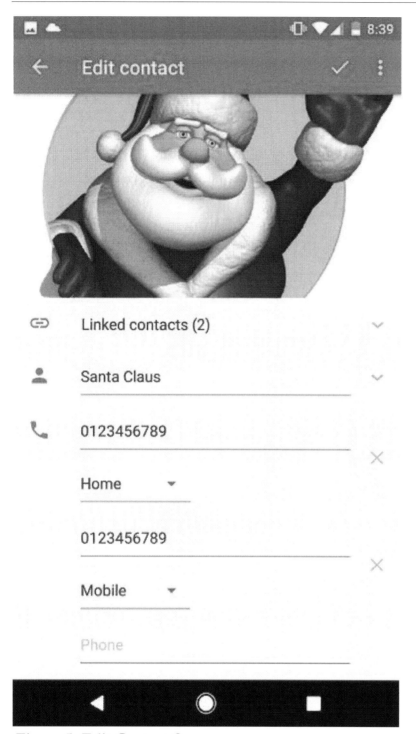

Figure 5: Edit Contact Screen

4. Deleting a Contact

Free up memory on the phone by deleting unneeded contacts from the phonebook. To delete a contact:

Warning: Contacts cannot be retrieved once they are deleted. Before deleting a contact, make sure that you do not need the information.

1. Touch the ![icon] icon on the Home screen or touch the bottom of any Home screen, slide up your finger, and touch the ![icon] icon. The Phonebook appears.
2. Touch and hold a contact's name. The contact is selected. Select any other contacts that you wish to delete. A ![checkmark] mark appears next to each selected contact.

3. Touch the ![trash icon] icon. A confirmation dialog appears.
4. Touch **DELETE**. The selected contacts are deleted.

5. Adding a Label to a Contact

Assign labels to contacts to make browsing for contacts easier. To add a label to a contact:

1. Touch the ![icon] icon on the Home screen or touch the bottom of any Home screen, slide up your finger, and touch the ![icon] icon. The Phonebook appears.
2. Touch the left-hand side of the screen, then slide your finger to the right. The Phonebook menu appears, as shown in **Figure 6**.
3. Touch a label. The Label screen appears, as shown in **Figure 7**.

4. Touch the ![icon] icon. The Phonebook appears.
5. Touch the name of a contact. The label is applied to the contact and the contact's name appears in the label list.

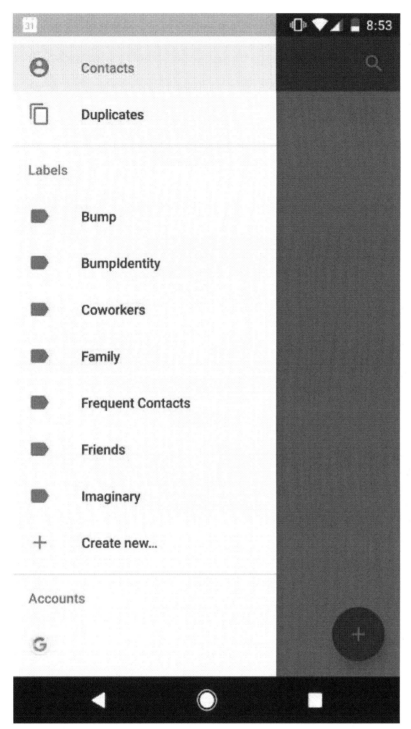

Figure 6: Phonebook Menu

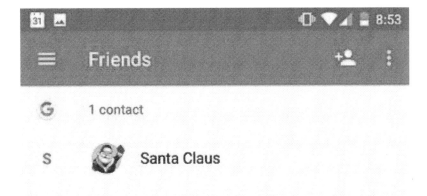

Figure 7: Label Screen

6. Adding a Contact to Favorites

The Favorites group can be used to quickly access the people that you contact the most often. To add a contact to Favorites:

1. Touch the icon on the Home screen or touch the bottom of any Home screen, slide up your finger, and touch the icon. The Phonebook appears.

2. Touch a contact's name. The contact's information appears.

3. Touch the icon at the top of the screen, as outlined in **Figure 8**. The contact is added to Favorites.

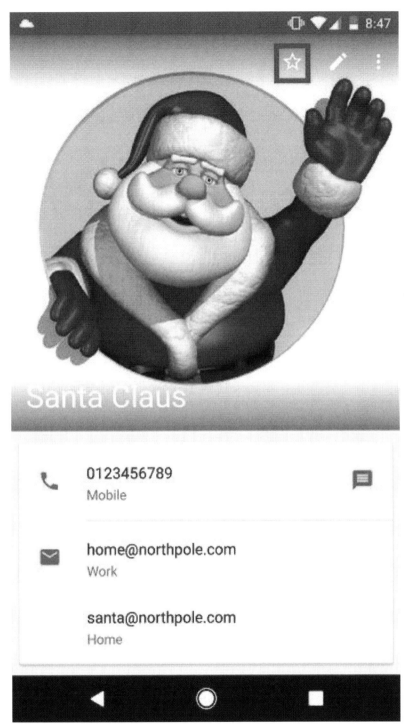

Figure 8: Favorites Icon Outlined

7. Sharing Contact Information via Email

When a contact is stored in the phonebook, all of the information for that contact is available in the form of a Namecard. A Namecard is a VCF file (opened with Outlook or a similar program) that can be shared with others, which conveniently transfers all of the contact's information to other phones. To share contact information:

1. Touch the [icon] icon on the Home screen or touch the bottom of any Home screen, slide up your finger, and touch the [icon] icon. The Phonebook appears.
2. Touch a contact's name. The contact's information appears.
3. Touch the [icon] icon at the top of the screen. The Contact menu appears.
4. Touch **Share**. The Sharing Method menu appears, as shown in **Figure 9**. The sharing methods vary based on the applications that you have installed on your phone.
5. Touch **Gmail** (recommended). A new message appears with the Namecard attached, as shown in **Figure 10**.
6. Enter an email address, subject, and optional message by touching each field. The information is entered. Refer to *"Writing an Email"* on page 163 to learn more about composing emails.
7. Touch the [icon] button in the upper right-hand corner of the screen. The email is sent and the contact information is shared. On a mobile phone, the recipient can save the Namecard directly to the Phonebook.

Note: Sharing contact information via Bluetooth is not covered in this guide due to its complexity and the fact that phones often fail to communicate with one another properly.

Figure 9: Sharing Method Menu

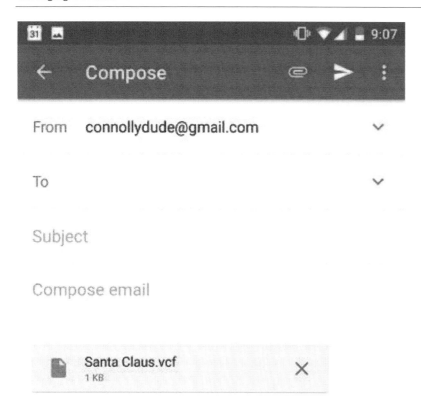

Figure 10: New Message with Attached Namecard

8. Changing the Contact Sorting Method

By default, contacts in the phonebook are sorted alphabetically by first name. For example, John Diss is listed before Ray Beeze because John comes before Ray in the alphabet. The last name is disregarded when sorting, unless there is more than one person with the same first name, in which case it is used to determine which name is listed first. To change the way contacts are sorted:

1. Touch the ![icon] icon on the Home screen or touch the bottom of any Home screen, slide up your finger, and touch the ![icon] icon. The Phonebook appears.
2. Touch the left-hand side of the screen and slide your finger to the right. The Phonebook menu appears.
3. Touch **Settings**. The Phonebook Settings screen appears, as shown in **Figure 11**.
4. Touch **Sort by**. The Sorting window appears.
5. Touch **Last name**. The contacts in the phonebook will now be sorted according to their last name. Using the example in this section, Ray Beeze would now come before John Diss. Repeat steps 1-5 and touch **First Name** to switch back to the default sorting method.

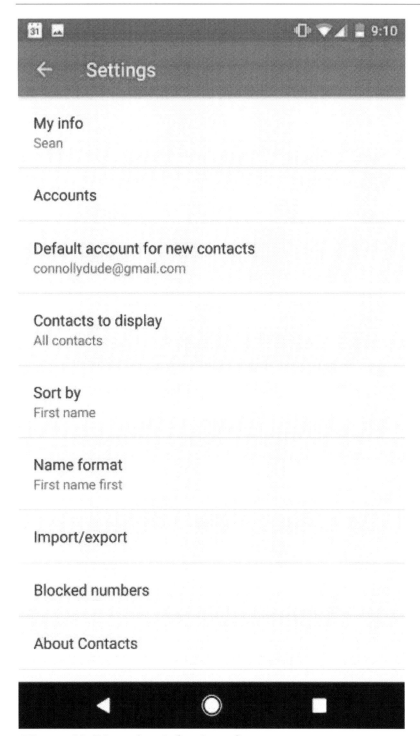

Figure 11: Phonebook Settings Screen

9. Changing the Contact Display Method

By default, contacts in the phonebook are displayed with the first name appearing first. For example, Sarah Bellum is displayed as "Sarah Bellum." To change the way contacts are displayed:

1. Touch the icon on the Home screen or touch the bottom of any Home screen, slide up your finger, and touch the icon. The Phonebook appears.
2. Touch the left-hand side of the screen and slide your finger to the right. The Phonebook menu appears.
3. Touch **Settings**. The Phonebook Settings screen appears.
4. Touch **Name format**. The Contact Display window appears.
5. Touch **Last name first**. Contacts will now be displayed with the last name appearing first. Using the example in this section, Sarah Bellum will now be displayed as "Bellum, Sarah." Repeat steps 1-5 and touch **First Name** to switch back to the default display method.

Using the Chrome Web Browser

Table of Contents

1. Navigating to a Website

One way to visit a website is to enter its web address in the Address bar. To navigate to a website using its web address:

1. Touch the icon on the Home screen, or touch the bottom of any Home screen and slide up your finger, then touch the icon. The Chrome browser opens.
2. Touch the Address bar at the top of the screen, as outlined in Figure 1. The Address bar is selected and the keyboard appears.
3. Enter a web address and touch the button. Chrome navigates to the website.

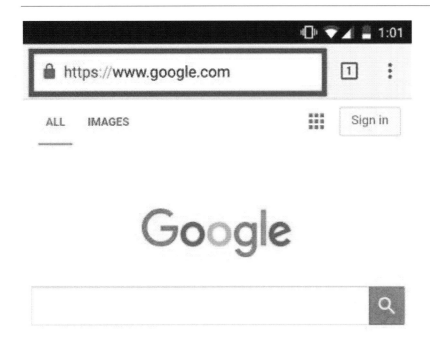

Figure 1: Address Bar Outlined

2. Adding and Viewing Bookmarks

The phone can store websites as bookmarks to access them faster. These bookmarks will appear on both your mobile devices and the computers that are logged in to your Google account in the Chrome browser. To add a bookmark:

1. Navigate to a website. Refer to *"Navigating to a Website"* on page 196 to learn how.
2. Touch the ⋮ icon in the Address bar. The Chrome menu appears, as shown in **Figure 2**.
3. Touch the ☆ icon. The page is saved to your bookmarks.

To view your bookmarks:

1. Touch the ⋮ icon in the upper right-hand corner of the browser. The Chrome menu appears.
2. Touch **Bookmarks**. The Bookmarks screen appears, as shown in **Figure 3**.
3. Touch a bookmark. Chrome navigates to the selected web page.

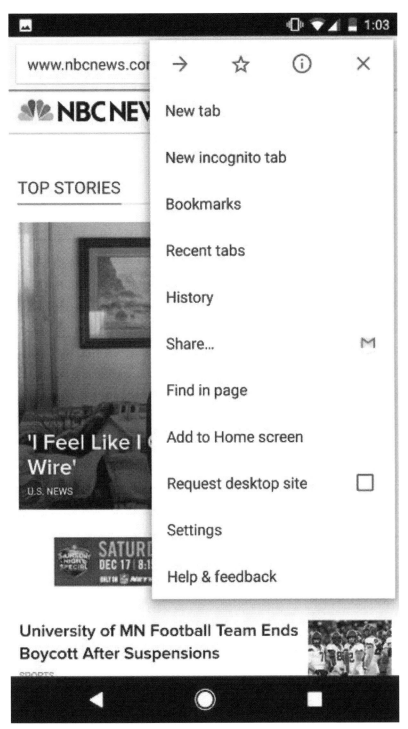

Figure 2: Chrome Menu

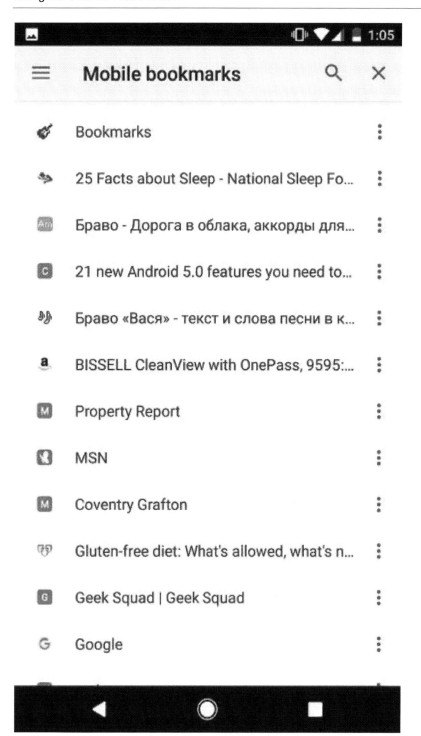

Figure 3: Bookmarks Screen

3. Editing and Deleting Bookmarks

Bookmarks may be edited if a new web address or label is desired. Bookmarks may also be deleted to free up space.

To edit a bookmark:

1. Touch the ⋮ icon in the upper right-hand corner of the browser. The Chrome menu appears.
2. Touch **Bookmarks**. The Bookmarks screen appears.
3. Touch and hold a bookmark. The Bookmark menu appears, as shown in **Figure 4**.
4. Touch the ✎ icon. The Bookmark Editing screen appears.
5. Touch a field to change the information. The bookmark is edited.
6. Touch the ◀ key. The new bookmark information is stored.

To delete a bookmark:

Warning: Once a bookmark is deleted, it is gone forever. There is no confirmation dialog when deleting a bookmark. Make sure that you wish to delete the bookmark before touching* Delete Bookmark *in step 4.

1. Touch the ⋮ icon in the upper right-hand corner of the browser. The Chrome menu appears.
2. Touch **Bookmarks**. The Bookmarks screen appears.
3. Touch and hold a bookmark. The Bookmark menu appears.
4. Touch the 🗑 icon. The bookmark is deleted.

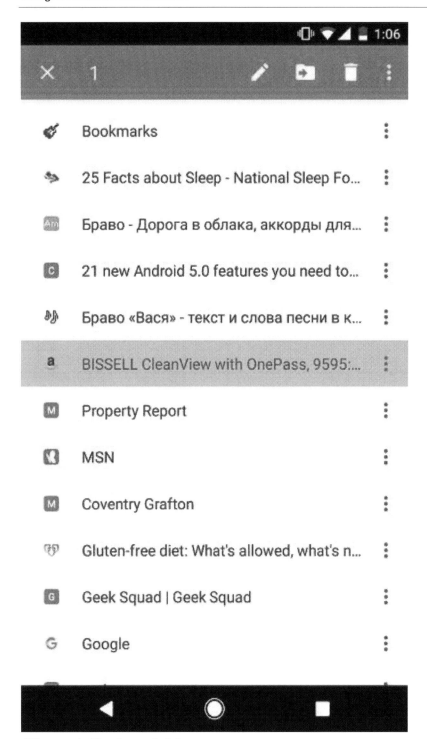

Figure 4: Bookmark Menu

4. Opening More than One Website at a Time

The Chrome browser allows you to have more than one web page opened at once, using separate tabs. The number of tabs that may be opened simultaneously is unlimited. Use the following tips to manage Chrome tabs:

- To add a tab, touch the ⦙ icon, and then touch **New tab**.

- To view an open Web page, touch the ⬜ icon, which contains the number of tabs that are currently open, then touch the tab that you would like to open.

- To close a tab, touch the ⬜ key, which contains the number of tabs that are currently open, then slide the tab that you want to close to the left or right.

5. Working with Links

In addition to touching a link to navigate to its destination, there are other link options. Touch and hold a link to see all link options, as follows:

- **Open in new tab** - Opens the link in a new tab, so as not lose the current Web page. Refer to *"Opening More than One Website at a Time"* on page 203 to learn how to view other open pages.
- **Open in Incognito tab** - Opens the link in a new Incognito tab, which will prevent you from leaving a trail in the form of a Web History while browsing in the tab.
- **Copy link address** - Copies the Web address to the clipboard.
- **Copy link text** - Copies the link as text rather than a hyperlink that can be clicked.
- **Download link** - Downloads the Web page to the phone. The Web page can then be

  accessed by sliding up your finger on the Home screen, then touching the ⬇ icon. The phone does not need to be connected to a Wi-Fi network to access the saved Web page, but it does need an internet connection if you wish to navigate to any of the links that it contains (if applicable).

6. Copying and Pasting Text

Text on any web page can be selected, copied, and pasted to another location. To copy and paste text:

1. Touch the beginning of the text until a word is highlighted in blue and the and ⬤ markers appear.

2. Touch and drag the ⬤ and ⬤ markers to select as much text as desired. The Text menu appears, as outlined in **Figure 5**.

3. Touch **COPY**. The text is copied to the clipboard. You can also touch **SELECT ALL** to select all of the text on the page.

4. To paste the text to another location, such as another application, touch and hold a text field. Touch **Paste**. The text is pasted to the new location.

Figure 5: Text Menu

7. Searching a Web Page for a Word or Phrase

While using the Chrome application, any Web page can be searched for a word or phrase. To perform a search of a Web page:

1. Touch the ⦂ icon in the upper right-hand corner of the screen. The Chrome menu appears.
2. Touch **Find in page**. The 'Find in page' field appears at the top of the screen, as shown in **Figure 6**.

3. Enter search keywords and touch the (Q) button. All matching search results are highlighted on the page, as shown in **Figure 7**.
4. Touch one of the yellow stripes on the right-hand side of the screen, as outlined in **Figure 7**, to navigate to a specific result. The result is highlighted in orange on the page.

Note: You can also touch the ⌃ or ⌄ icons to the right of the Search field to navigate to the previous or next result, respectively.

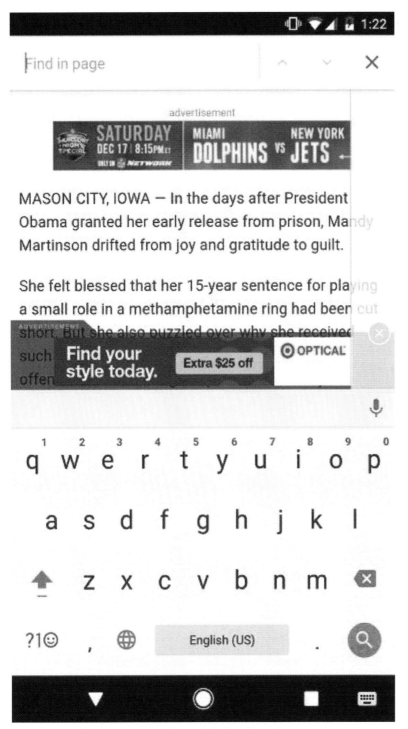

Figure 6: 'Find in Page' Field Outlined

Figure 7: Matching Search Results Highlighted in Yellow

8. Viewing the Most Recently Visited Websites

The phone stores all recently visited websites. To view the most recently visited sites:

1. Touch the ⋮ icon in the upper right-hand corner of the browser. The Chrome menu appears.
2. Touch **Recent tabs**. The Bookmarks screen appears. The most recently visited sites appear, as shown in **Figure 8**.
3. Touch a site in the list. Chrome navigates to the web page.

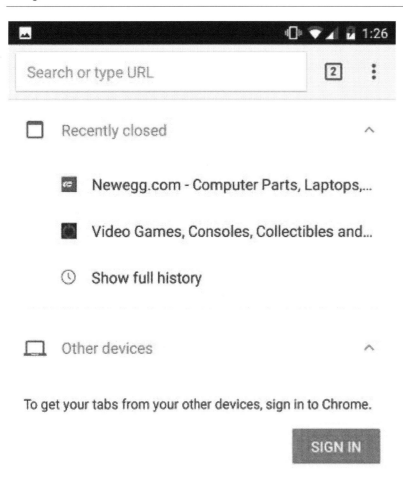

Figure 8: Most Recently Visited Sites

9. Automatically Filling in Online Forms

The Autofill feature can automatically enter your personal information into online forms by using a predefined Autofill profile. To add a new Autofill profile:

1. Touch the ⋮ icon in the upper right-hand corner of the browser. The Chrome menu appears.
2. Touch **Settings**. The Chrome Settings screen appears.
3. Touch **Autofill forms**. The Autofill Profiles screen appears, as shown in **Figure 9**.
4. Touch the ⋮ icon next to **Addresses** or **Credit cards**. The Add Address or Add Credit Card screen appears.
5. Touch each field to enter the associated information. Then, touch **Done**. The Autofill profile is saved and the information that you provided will be automatically entered into online forms.

Note: Refer to "Clearing the Data that is Used to Speed Up Browsing" *on page 221 to learn how to delete all saved forms.*

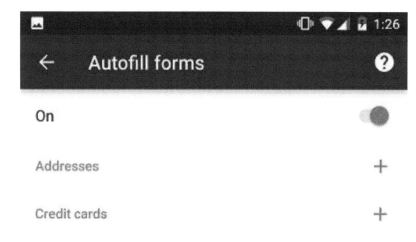

Figure 9: Autofill Profiles Screen

10. Saving and Managing Passwords for Websites

The Chrome browser can save your account credentials for various websites, such as email clients and shopping sites. By default, Chrome offers to save a password when you enter it. In order to protect your privacy, you may also delete saved passwords for specific websites after they have been stored.

To enable the saving of usernames and passwords:

1. Touch the ⋮ icon in the upper right-hand corner of the browser. The Chrome menu appears.
2. Touch **Settings**. The Chrome Settings screen appears.
3. Touch **Save passwords**. The Saved Passwords screen appears, as shown in **Figure 10**.
4. Touch the ⬤ switch at the top of the screen. The ⬤ switch appears and Chrome will no longer offer to save passwords.
5. Touch the ⬤ switch. The ⬤ switch appears and Chrome will offer to save passwords every time that you enter one.

To delete a stored password for a specific website:

1. Follow steps 1-3 above. The Saved Passwords screen appears.
2. Touch a website under **Passwords**. The Saved Password URL and email to which the account is assigned appear, as shown in **Figure 11**.
3. Touch **Delete**. The saved password for the website is deleted.

Note: Refer to *"Clearing the Data that is Used to Speed Up Browsing"* on page 221 to learn how to delete all saved passwords at once.

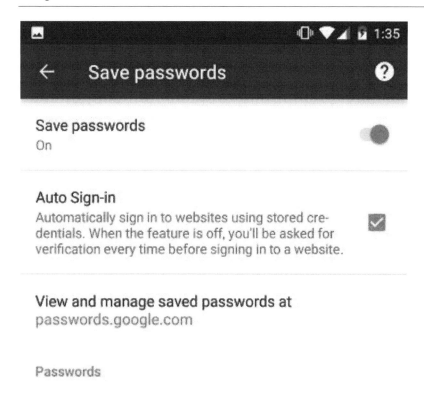

Figure 10: Saved Passwords Screen

thehelpmeguide@gmail.com

facebook.com

Figure 11: Saved Password URL

11. Setting the Search Engine

Google, Yahoo, Bing, Ask, or AOL may be used as the default search engine in the Chrome browser. To perform a search at any time, enter a search term in the Address bar. Refer to *"Navigating to a Website"* on page 196 to locate the Address bar. To set the search engine:

1. Touch the ⋮ icon in the upper right-hand corner of the browser. The Chrome menu appears.
2. Touch **Settings**. The Chrome Settings screen appears.
3. Touch **Search engine**. A list of available search engines appears.
4. Touch a search engine. The search engine is selected and will be used whenever a search is performed.

12. Setting the Font Size

The text size used in the Chrome browser can be changed. To set the browser's font size:

1. Touch the ⋮ icon in the upper right-hand corner of the browser. The Chrome menu appears.
2. Touch **Settings**. The Chrome Settings screen appears.
3. Touch **Accessibility**. The Chrome Accessibility Settings screen appears, as shown in **Figure 12**.
4. Touch the **Text Scaling** slider and drag it to the left or right to decrease or increase the font size, respectively. The font size is adjusted and will be used on all websites.

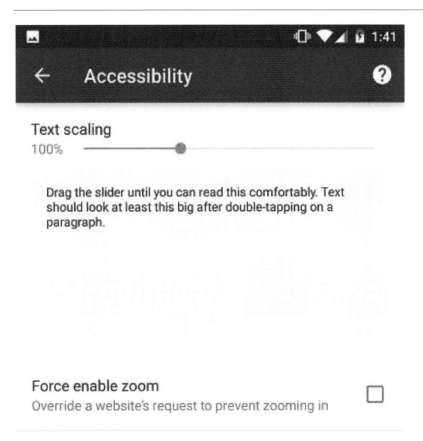

Figure 12: Chrome Accessibility Settings Screen

13. Blocking Pop-Up Windows

Some websites may cause pop-up windows to appear, interfering with your browsing. By default, pop-ups are blocked. To prevent pop-up windows:

1. Touch the ⋮ icon in the upper right-hand corner of the browser. The Chrome menu appears.
2. Touch **Settings**. The Chrome Settings screen appears.
3. Touch **Site settings**. The Site Settings screen appears, as shown in **Figure 13**.
4. Touch **Pop-ups**. The Pop-ups screen appears.
5. Touch **Pop-ups**. 'Pop-ups Allowed' appears, and pop-ups are turned on.
6. Touch **Pop-ups**. 'Pop-ups Blocked' appears, and pop-ups are turned off.

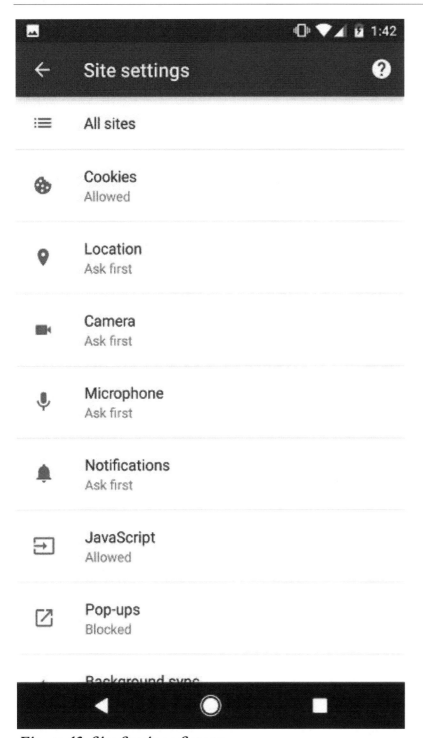

Figure 13: Site Settings Screen

14. Recalling Sites More Quickly on Subsequent Visits

The Chrome browser can store data that is used to quickly recall sites that you have previously visited, called Cookies. This feature provides convenience, but may also take up some space on your phone. By default, the Chrome browser stores these data. To recall sites faster on subsequent visits:

1. Touch the ⋮ icon in the upper right-hand corner of the browser. The Chrome menu appears.
2. Touch **Settings**. The Chrome Settings screen appears.
3. Touch **Site settings**. The Content Settings screen appears.
4. Touch **Cookies**. The ⬤ switch appears and Chrome will not store data that will help to recall sites faster on subsequent visits.
5. Touch **Cookies** again. The ⬤ switch appears and Chrome will save data that will help to recall sites faster on subsequent visits.

Note: Refer to "Clearing the Data that is Used to Speed Up Browsing" *on page 221 to learn how to delete Cookies.*

15. Turning JavaScript On or Off

JavaScript is used primarily for animation and interactive elements on websites, as with games, audio, and video. Turning on JavaScript will allow you to view such content, but may slow down the loading process when you visit sites that contain it. By default, JavaScript is turned on. To turn JavaScript on or off:

1. Touch the ⋮ icon in the upper right-hand corner of the browser. The Chrome menu appears.
2. Touch **Settings**. The Chrome Settings screen appears.
3. Touch **Site settings**. The Content Settings screen appears.
4. Touch **JavaScript**. The ⬤ mark appears and JavaScript is turned on.
5. Touch **JavaScript** again. The ⬤ switch appears and JavaScript is turned off.

16. Clearing the Data that is Used to Speed Up Browsing

Chrome stores data, which allows it to load previously visited websites and fill in forms more quickly. In order to protect your privacy, you may wish to delete these data. To clear some or all of the data that is used to speed up browsing:

1. Touch the ⋮ icon in the upper right-hand corner of the browser. The Chrome menu appears.
2. Touch **Settings**. The Chrome Settings screen appears.
3. Touch **Privacy**. The Privacy Settings screen appears, as shown in **Figure 14**.
4. Touch the ⋮ icon at the top of the screen. The Privacy Menu appears.
5. Touch **Clear Browsing Data**. A list of browsing data types appears, as shown in **Figure 15**.
6. Touch one of the following options to select the type of data for deletion:
    - **Browsing history** - Deletes all history files, including the addresses of recently visited websites.
    - **Cached images and files** - Deletes all Web page data, such as images and other files that comprise a website.
    - **Cookies and site data** - Deletes all text data, such as site preferences, authentication, or shopping cart contents.
    - **Saved passwords** - Deletes all stored passwords for various websites, such as email clients, marketplaces, and banking sites.
    - **Autofill form data** - Deletes all form data, including screen names, addresses, phone numbers, and more.
7. Touch **CLEAR DATA**. The selected data is deleted.

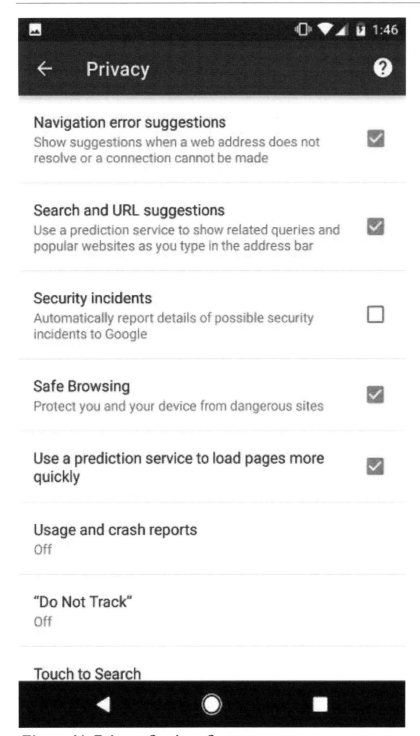

Figure 14: Privacy Settings Screen

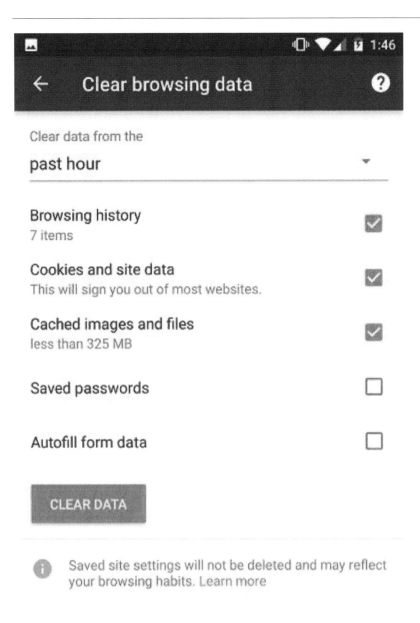

Figure 15: List of Browsing Data Types

17. Turning Suggestions for Searches and Web Addresses On or Off

While you enter a Web address or search query in the Address bar, Chrome can automatically make suggestions based on other popular choices. To set Chrome to show suggestions when you enter a search query:

1. Touch the ⋮ icon in the upper right-hand corner of the browser. The Chrome menu appears.
2. Touch **Settings**. The Chrome Settings screen appears
3. Touch **Privacy**. The Privacy Settings screen appears.
4. Touch **Search and URL suggestions**. The ✓ mark appears and Chrome will make suggestions when you perform a search or enter a Web address.
5. Touch **Search and URL suggestions** again. The ✓ mark disappears and Chrome will not make suggestions for searches and Web addresses.

Wireless Settings

Table of Contents

1. Turning Airplane Mode On or Off

Putting the phone in Airplane mode turns off all wireless communications, including Wi-Fi. Use Airplane mode to save battery life or while flying. To turn on Airplane mode:

1. Touch the status bar at the top of the screen with two fingers and slide down. The Quick Settings appear, as shown in **Figure 1**.

2. Touch the icon. Airplane Mode turns on and all wireless communications are turned off.

3. Touch the icon. Airplane Mode turns off and all wireless communications are turned on.

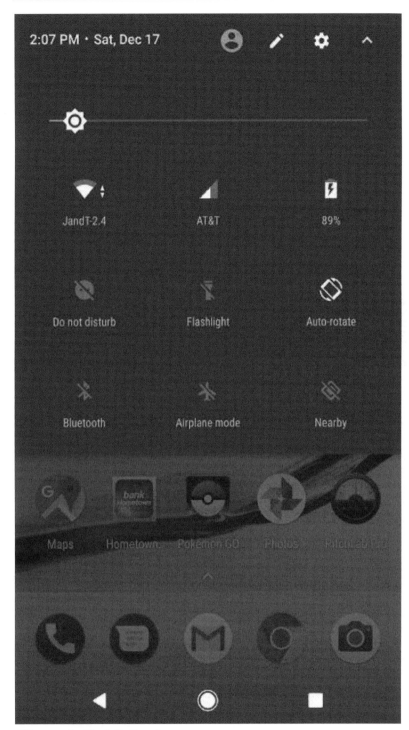

Figure 1: Quick Settings

2. Connecting to a Wi-Fi Network

The phone can connect to Wi-Fi when it is near a hotspot or a wireless network. To connect to a Wi-Fi network:

1. Touch the status bar at the top of the screen with two fingers and slide down. The Quick Settings appear.

2. Touch and hold the ▼ icon. The Wi-Fi screen appears.
3. Touch **Off** if Wi-Fi is turned off. A list of available Wi-Fi networks appears, as shown in **Figure 2**.
4. Touch the name of a network. If the network is secured, the Wi-Fi Network Password prompt appears, as shown in **Figure 3**.
5. Enter the network password (usually found on your wireless router) and touch **Connect**. The phone connects to the network, provided that the password you entered is correct. If the password is incorrect, 'Authenticating' appears next to the name of the network indefinitely.

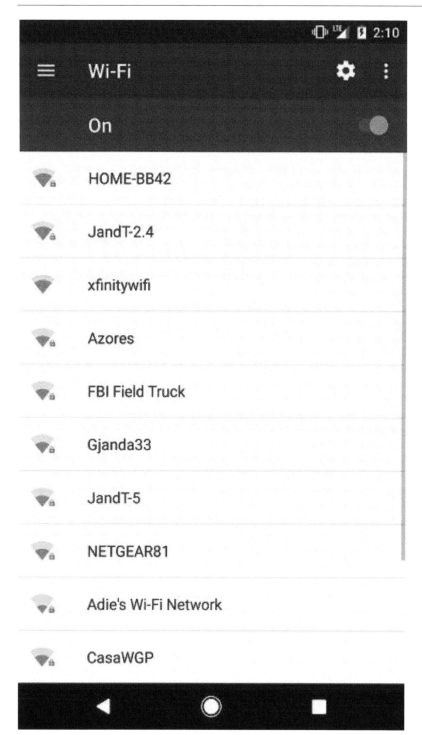

Figure 2: List of Available Wi-Fi Networks

Figure 3: Network Password Prompt

3. Using Bluetooth

Bluetooth allows the phone to communicate with phones, tablets, and other wireless devices. To turn on Bluetooth and pair with another device:

1. Touch the status bar at the top of the screen with two fingers and slide down. The Quick Settings appear.

2. Touch and hold the ![icon] icon. The Wi-Fi screen appears.

3. Touch **Off** if Bluetooth is turned off. The ![switch] switch appears and Bluetooth is turned on. A list of devices appears, which are in close proximity to the phone and also have their Bluetooth turned on, as shown in **Figure 4**. Make sure that the secondary device is ready to pair.

4. Touch a device in the list. The Bluetooth Pairing Request window appears. The phone is paired with the secondary device. To turn off Bluetooth, touch **On** at the top of the screen.

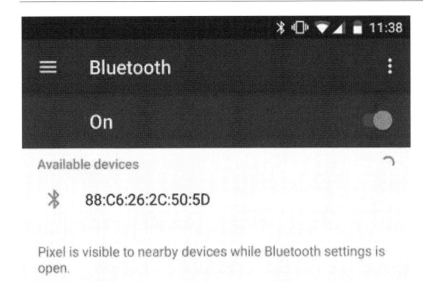

Available devices

88:C6:26:2C:50:5D

Pixel is visible to nearby devices while Bluetooth settings is open.

Figure 4: List of Bluetooth Devices

4. Wirelessly Transferring Data to Another phone

The phone can transfer data to another mobile phone without the use of Bluetooth or email. By using the Android Beam feature, you can transfer data by holding your phone back to back with another Android Beam-enabled phone. To wirelessly transfer data using the Android Beam feature:

1. Touch the bottom of any Home screen, then slide up your finger. Touch the icon. The Settings screen appears, as shown in **Figure 5**.

2. Touch **More** under Wireless & networks. The Additional Wireless settings appear, as shown in **Figure 6**.

3. Touch **NFC**. The ⬤ switch appears and NFC is turned on.

4. Touch **Android Beam**. The Android Beam screen appears, as shown in **Figure 7**.

5. Touch **Off** at the top of the screen. The ⬤ switch appears and the Android Beam feature is turned on. You are now ready to wirelessly transfer data.

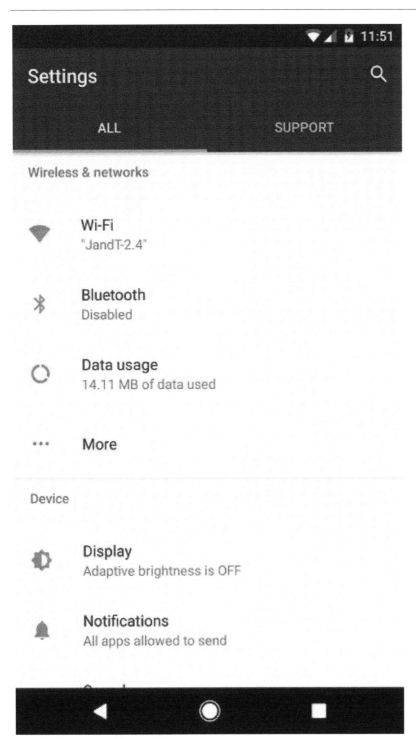

Figure 5: Settings Screen

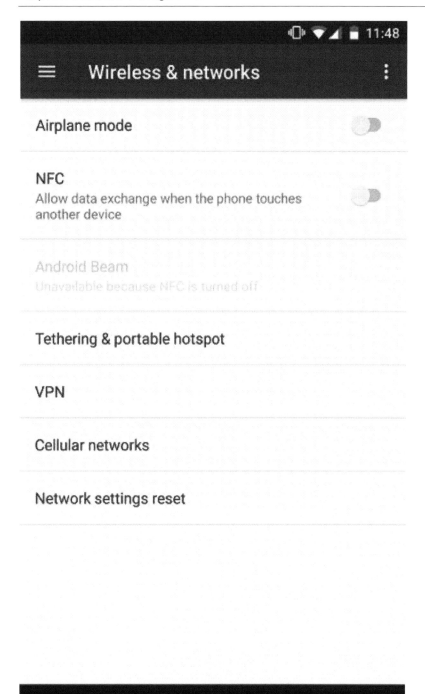

Figure 6: Additional Wireless Settings

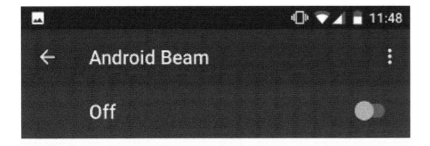

When this feature is turned on, you can beam app content to another NFC-capable device by holding the devices close together. For example, you can beam Browser pages, YouTube videos, People contacts, and more.

Just bring the devices together (typically back to back) and then tap your screen. The app determines what gets beamed.

Figure 7: Android Beam Screen

5. Turning Cellular Data On or Off

In an area where there is little to no reception, you may want to turn off cellular data and connect to a wireless network. When you are connected to a Wi-Fi network, cellular data is not used to download applications or stream media. However, the phone will keep searching for a signal, which drains the battery very quickly. To turn cellular data on or off:

1. Touch the status bar at the top of the screen with two fingers and slide down. The Quick Settings appear.
2. Touch the 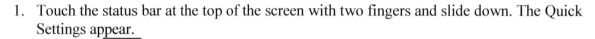 icon. The Cellular Data window appears, as shown in **Figure 8**.
3. Touch **Cellular data** at the top of the screen. The ◯ switch appears and cellular data is turned off.
4. Touch **Cellular data** again. The ◯ switch appears, and cellular data is turned on.

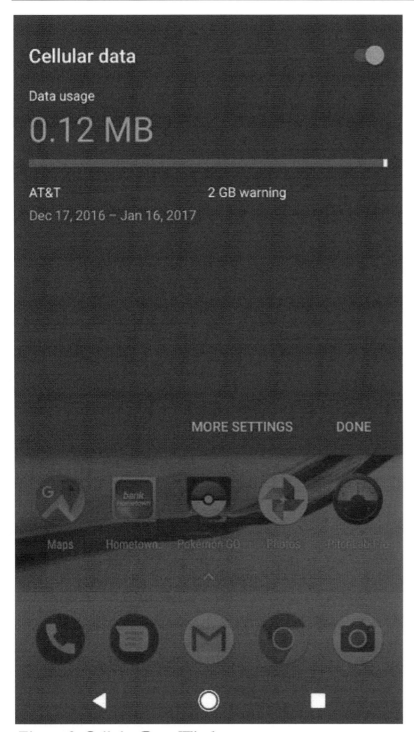

Figure 8: Cellular Data Window

Sound Settings

Table of Contents

1. Adjusting the Notification, Media, and Alarm Volume

The volume for various notifications can be set separately. To set the various Notification volume:

1. Touch the bottom of any Home screen, then slide up your finger. Touch the icon. The Settings screen appears, as shown in **Figure 1**. Refer to *"Tips and Tricks"* on page 296 to learn how to quickly access the Settings screen.
2. Touch Sound. The Sound settings appear, as shown in **Figure 2**.
3. Touch one of the sliders and drag it to the left or right to decrease or increase the corresponding Notification volume, respectively. The volume is adjusted.

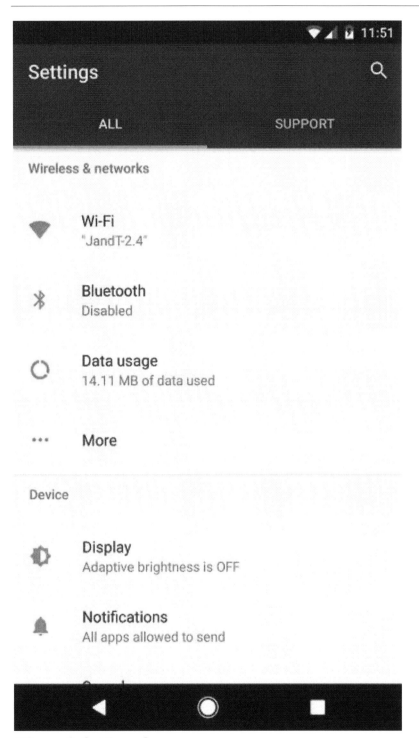

Figure 1: Settings Screen

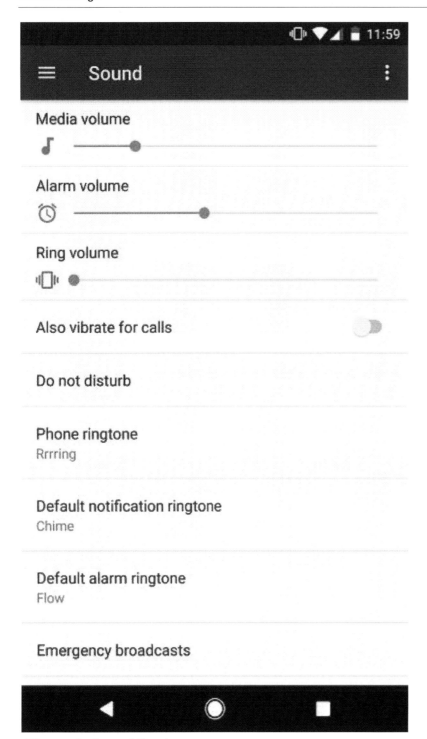

Figure 2: Sound Settings

2. Changing the Ringtones

The default ringtone that is used for all notifications can be changed. To set the Notification ringtone:

1. Touch the bottom of any Home screen, then slide up your finger. Touch the icon. The Settings screen appears.
2. Touch **Sound**. The Sound Settings screen appears.
3. Touch **Phone ringtone**, **Default notification ringtone**, or **Default alarm ringtone** to set the corresponding ringtone. A list of Notification ringtones appears.
4. Touch a ringtone. A preview of the ringtone plays.
5. Touch **OK**. The new ringtone is set. Alternatively, touch **Cancel** to return to continue using the previously set ringtone.

3. Turning System Sounds On or Off

When any selection is made on the touchscreen, the phone can play a confirmation sound. To turn Touch Sounds on or off:

1. Touch the bottom of any Home screen, then slide up your finger. Touch the icon. The Settings screen appears.
2. Touch Sound & notification. The Sound Settings screen appears.
3. Touch Other sounds. The Other Sounds settings appear, as shown in **Figure 3**.
4. Touch one of the following options in the list. The switch appears next to any sound that is turned on. The switch appears next to any sound that is turned off.
    - **Dial pad tones** - Sounds that are played when you touch the keys on the phone keypad.
    - **Screen locking sounds** - Sounds that are played every time that you lock or unlock the phone.
    - **Charge sounds** - Sounds that are played every time that you plug in or unplug the charging cable.
    - **Touch sounds** - Sounds that are played every time that you touch a selection in a menu

- **Vibrate on tap** - Vibrations that are made every time that you touch the , , or key.

- **Power on sounds** - Sounds that are played every time that you turn on the phone.

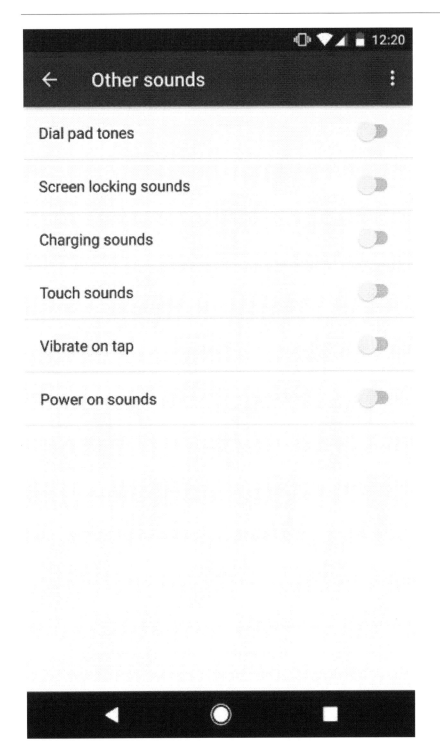

Figure 3: Other Sounds Settings

Screen Settings

Table of Contents

1. Adjusting the Brightness

The phone can be set to automatically detect light conditions by using the built-in light sensor, and then set the brightness accordingly. When Adaptive Brightness is turned off, you may manually adjust the brightness. To customize the brightness:

1. Touch the bottom of any Home screen, then slide up your finger. Touch the icon. The Settings screen appears, as shown in **Figure 1**.
2. Touch **Display**. The Display Settings screen appears, as shown in **Figure 2**.
3. Touch **Brightness level**. The Brightness slider appears.
4. Touch and drag the slider to the left or right. The brightness is decreased or increased, respectively. You can also touch Adaptive brightness to enable the phone to automatically adjust the brightness based on lighting conditions.

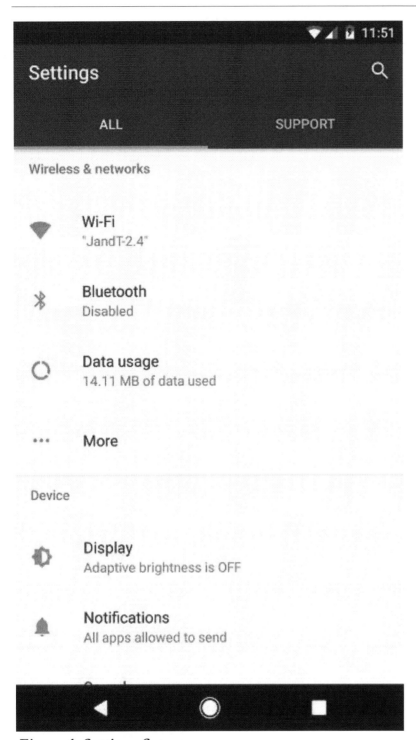

Figure 1: Settings Screen

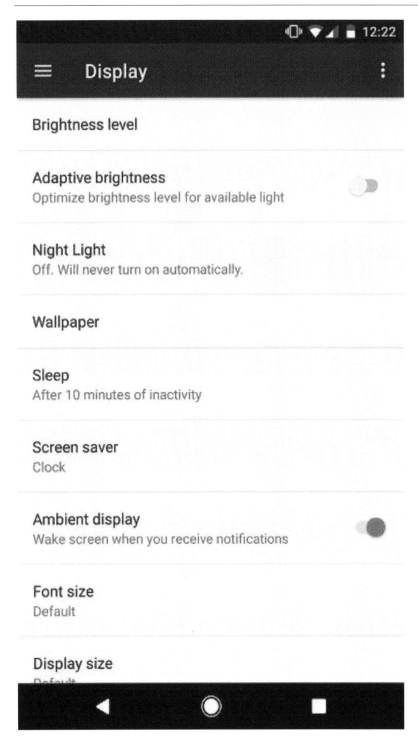

Figure 2: Display Settings Screen

2. Turning Automatic Screen Rotation On or Off

By default, the screen rotates every time the phone is rotated from the horizontal to the vertical position and vice versa (except when viewing a Home screen). To turn Automatic Screen Rotation on or off:

1. Touch the status bar at the top of the screen with two fingers and slide down. The Quick Settings appear, as shown in **Figure 3**.

2. Touch the 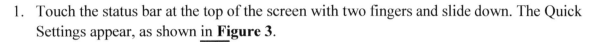 icon. The icon appears and Automatic Screen Rotation is turned off.

3. Touch the 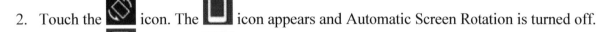 icon. The icon appears and Automatic Screen Rotation is turned on.

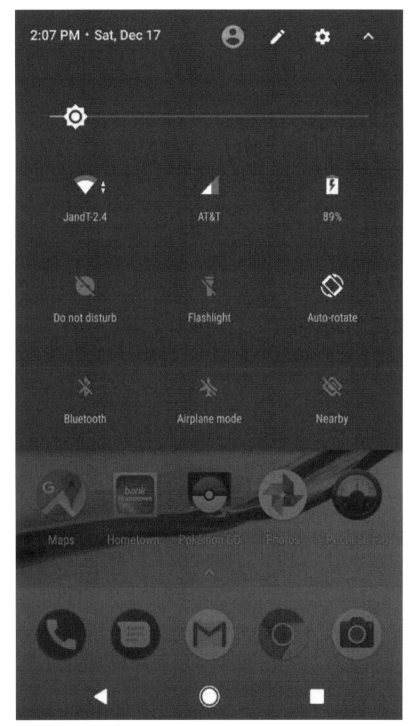

Figure 3: Quick Settings Menu

3. Changing the Wallpaper

The wallpaper is the image that is displayed in the background on the Lock and Home screens. To change the wallpaper:

1. Touch and hold an empty spot on any Home screen. The Home Screen menu appears, as shown in **Figure 4**.
2. Touch **Wallpapers**. Thumbnails for images in the corresponding source appear.
3. Touch the desired image, then touch Set wallpaper. You may need to crop the image before setting it as the wallpaper. Refer to *"Cropping a Picture"* on page 146 to learn how.

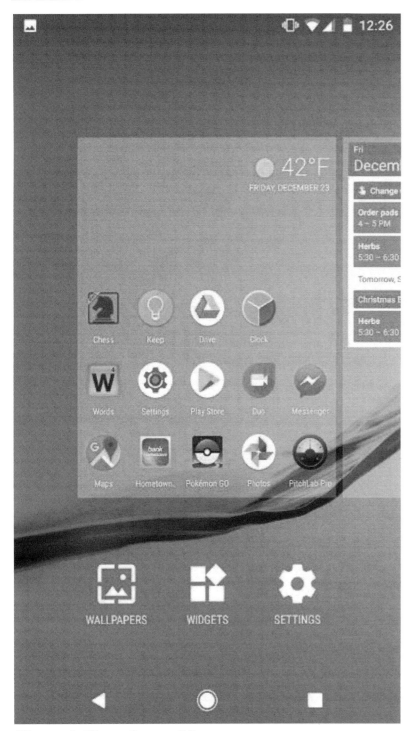

Figure 4: Home Screen Menu

4. Setting the Amount of Time Before the Phone Locks Itself

The Sleep Timer determines the amount of time that passes before the screen turns off and the phone is automatically locked. To set the Sleep Timer:

1. Touch the bottom of any Home screen, then slide up your finger. Touch the icon. The Settings screen appears.

2. Touch **Display**. The Display Settings screen appears.

3. Touch **Sleep**. The Sleep Timer options appear, as shown in **Figure 5**.

4. Touch an option in the list. The Sleep Timer is set.

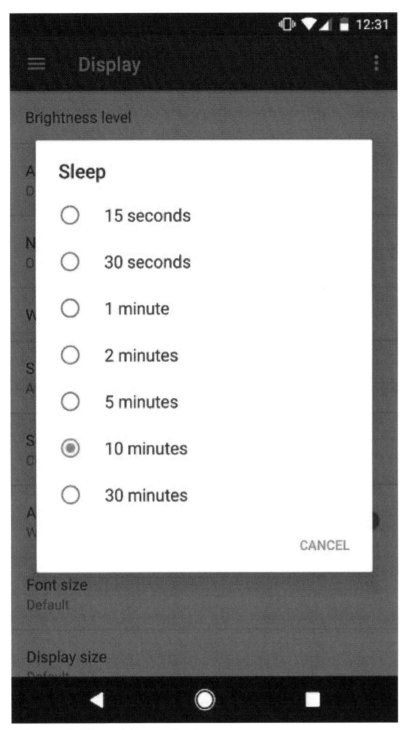

Figure 5: Sleep Timer Options

6. Adjusting the Font Size

If you have trouble seeing text in menus and applications, try increasing the font size. To adjust the font size on the phone:

1. Touch the icon on the Home screen, or touch the icon and then touch the icon. The Settings screen appears.

2. Touch **Display**. The Display Settings screen appears.

3. Touch **Font size**. The Font Size screen appears, as shown in **Figure 6**.

4. Touch one of the options in the list. The font size is adjusted.

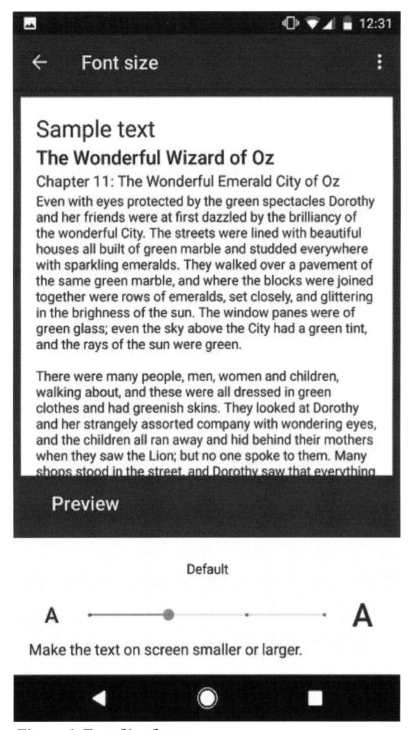

Figure 6: Font Size Screen

6. Customizing Contact Notification Priorities

You can customize notifications on the Pixel to help you avoid unnecessary interruptions when you are busy. First, set your 'Priority' contacts, for whom notifications will show when in Priority mode. To add the 'Priority' status to a contact:

1. Touch the ![icon] icon on the Home screen or touch the bottom of any Home screen, slide up your finger, and touch the ![icon] icon. The Phonebook appears, as shown in **Figure 7**.

2. Touch the name of the contact that you wish to edit. The contact's information appears, as shown in **Figure 8**.

3. Touch the ![star] icon. The Priority status is assigned to the contact.

To customize notifications:

1. Touch the top of the screen with two fingers and slide down. The Quick Settings.

2. Touch **Do Not Disturb**. The Do not disturb screen appears, as shown in **Figure 9**.

3. Touch **Priority Only**. The Priority Only options appear.

4. Touch **Until you turn this off** or **For one hour** to schedule Do Not Disturb. You can also touch the + and - buttons to adjust the time.

5. Touch **Done**. Do Not Disturb is turned on. To turn off Do Not Disturb, touch Priority only in the Quick Settings.

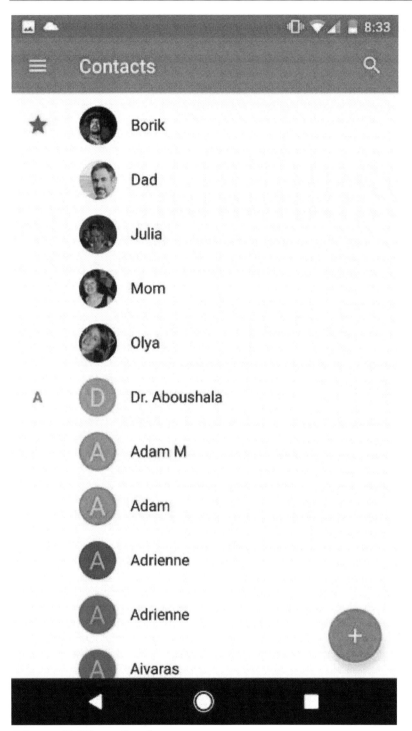

Figure 7: Phonebook

Figure 8: Contact Information

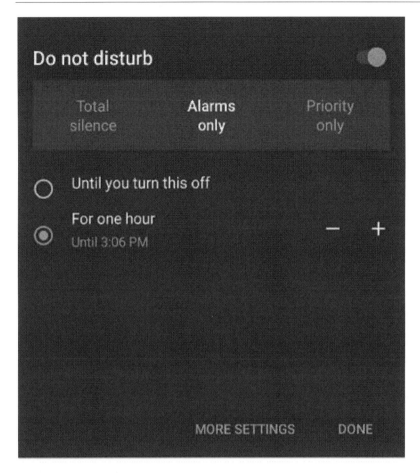

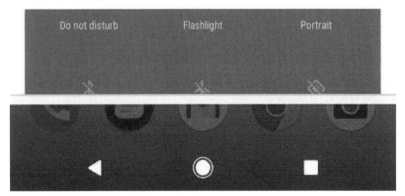

Figure 9: Do Not Disturb Screen

Security Settings

Table of Contents

1. Leaving the Screen Unlocked at All Times

If you do not want to have to slide your finger up on the screen or use a password, pattern, or fingerprint, you can set the phone to unlock as soon as you press the Power/Sleep button. Be aware that leaving the screen unlocked does not prevent unauthorized users from accessing your phone. To leave the screen unlocked at all times:

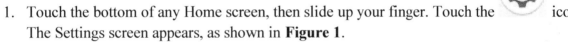

1. Touch the bottom of any Home screen, then slide up your finger. Touch the   icon. The Settings screen appears, as shown in **Figure 1**.
2. Touch **Security**. The Security Settings screen appears, as shown in **Figure 2**.
3. Touch **Screen lock**. The Screen Lock Settings screen appears, as shown in **Figure 3**.
4. Touch **None**. The screen will not be unlocked at all times.

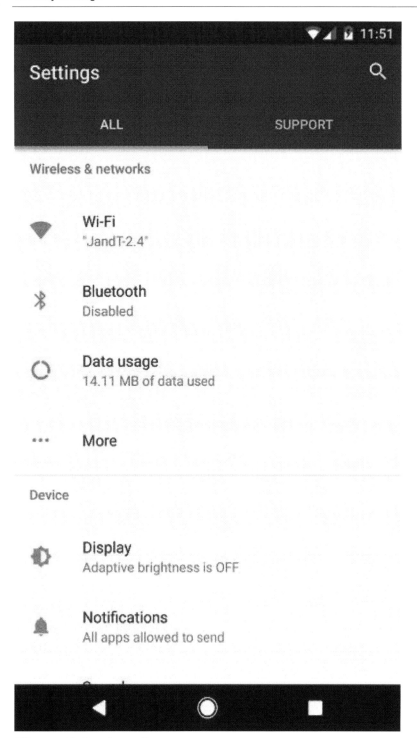

Figure 1: Settings Screen

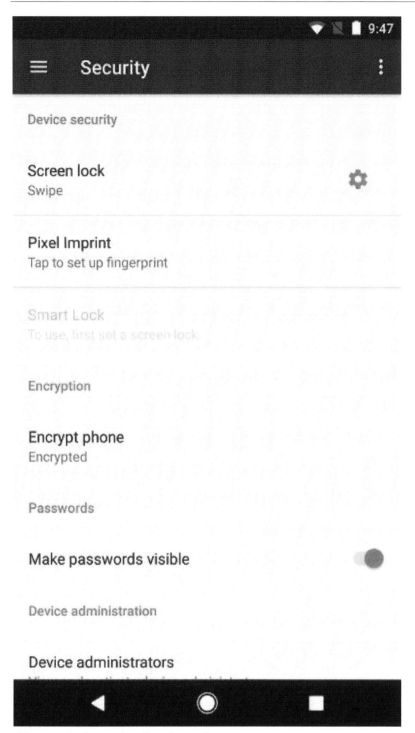

Figure 2: Security Settings Screen

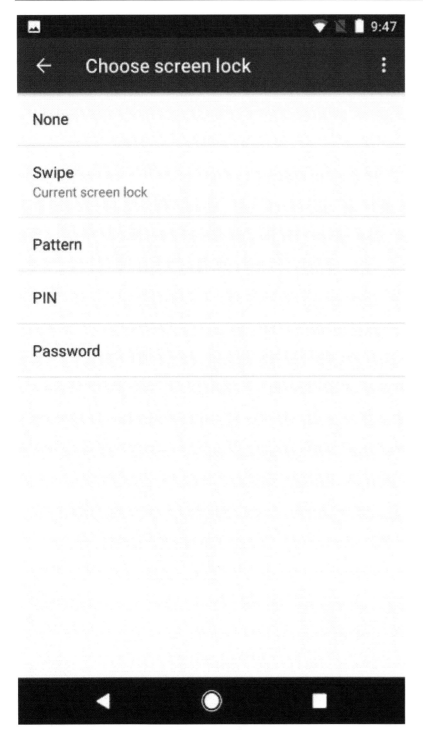

Figure 3: Screen Lock Settings Screen

2. Locking the Screen with Swipe

Prevent the phone from waking up accidentally by setting up a Swipe lock. Be aware that a Swipe lock does not prevent unauthorized users from accessing your phone. Refer to one of the next four sections to learn how to prevent unauthorized users from accessing your phone. To set up a Swipe lock:

1. Touch the bottom of any Home screen, then slide up your finger. Touch the   icon. The Settings screen appears.
2. Touch **Security**. The Security Settings screen appears.
3. Touch **Screen lock**. The Screen Lock Settings screen appears. If a screen lock has already been set up, you will need to enter the corresponding passcode or pattern before proceeding.
4. Touch **Swipe**. The phone will be locked using a basic swipe. To unlock it, touch the screen anywhere and slide your finger up. The phone is unlocked.

3. Locking the Screen with an Alphanumeric Password

In order to prevent unauthorized users from accessing your phone, you may wish to lock the phone using an alphanumeric (letters and numbers) password. To lock the screen using an alphanumeric password:

1. Touch the bottom of any Home screen, then slide up your finger. Touch the   icon. The Settings screen appears.

2. Touch **Security**. The Security Settings screen appears.

3. Touch **Screen lock**. The Screen Lock Settings screen appears. If a screen lock has already been set up, you will need to enter the corresponding passcode, PIN, or pattern before proceeding. The Choose Your Password screen appears, as shown in **Figure 4**.

4. Enter the desired password. The password must be at least four and no more than 16 characters in length. Touch Continue. The Password Confirmation screen appears.

5. Enter the same password again. Touch **OK**. The Notification Settings screen appears. This screen only appears if you are changing from a non-secure locking method to a PIN.

6. Touch one of the following options to configure notification behavior while the phone is locked with a password:

- **Show all notification content** - Displays all notifications while the phone is locked.

- **Hide sensitive notification content** - Displays only the name of the application that sent the notification, such as Messenger or Gmail, but does not display the contents of the notification.

- **Don't show notifications at all** - Hides all notifications while the phone is locked.

7. Touch **Done**. The Password lock is set. The password will now be required to unlock the screen.

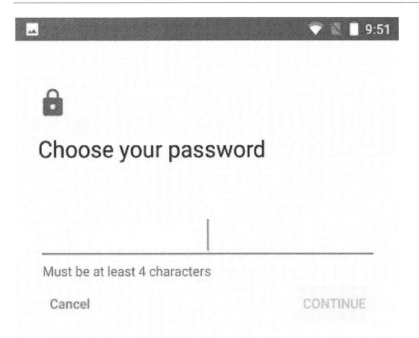

Figure 4: Choose Your Password Screen

4. Locking the Screen with a Personal Identification Number (PIN)

In order to prevent unauthorized users from accessing your phone, you may wish to lock the phone using a numerical PIN. To lock the screen using a PIN:

1. Touch the bottom of any Home screen, then slide up your finger. Touch the ⚙ icon. The Settings screen appears.

2. Touch **Security**. The Security Settings screen appears.

3. Touch **Screen lock**. The Screen Lock Settings screen appears. If a screen lock has already been set up, you will need to enter the corresponding passcode, PIN, or pattern before proceeding. The Choose Your PIN screen appears, as shown in **Figure 5**.

4. Enter the desired PIN, which must be at least 4 and no more than 16 digits in length. Touch Continue. The PIN Confirmation screen appears.

5. Enter the same PIN again. Touch **OK**. The Notification Settings screen appears. This screen only appears if you are changing from a non-secure locking method to a PIN.

6. Touch one of the following options to configure notification behavior while the phone is locked with a PIN:

   - **Show all notification content** - Displays all notifications while the phone is locked.

   - **Hide sensitive notification content** - Displays only the name of the application that sent the notification, such as Messenger or Gmail, but does not display the contents of the notification.

   - **Don't show notifications at all** - Hides all notifications while the phone is locked.

7. Touch **Done**. The PIN lock is set. The PIN will now be required to unlock the screen.

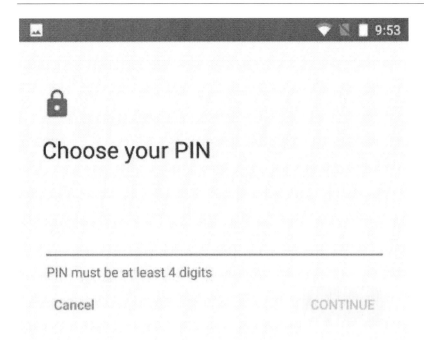

Figure 5: PIN Selection Screen

5. Locking the Screen with a Pattern

In order to prevent unauthorized users from accessing your phone, you may wish to lock the phone using a pattern. To lock the screen using a pattern:

1. Touch the bottom of any Home screen, then slide up your finger. Touch the ⚙ icon. The Settings screen appears.

2. Touch **Security**. The Security Settings screen appears.

3. Touch **Screen lock**. The Screen Lock Settings screen appears. If a screen lock has already been set up, you will need to enter the corresponding passcode, PIN, or pattern before proceeding.

4. Touch **Pattern**. The Encryption screen appears. The Choose Your Pattern screen appears, as shown in **Figure 6**.

5. Draw the desired pattern. You must connect at least four dots. Touch **Continue**. The Pattern Confirmation screen appears.

6. Draw the same pattern again. Touch **Confirm**. The Notification Settings screen appears. This screen only appears if you are changing from a non-secure locking method to a PIN.

7. Touch one of the following options to configure notification behavior while the phone is locked with a pattern:

    -   **Show all notification content** - Displays all notifications while the phone is locked.

    -   **Hide sensitive notification content** - Displays only the name of the application that sent the notification, such as Messenger or Gmail, but does not display the contents of the notification.

    -   **Don't show notifications at all** - Hides all notifications while the phone is locked.

8. Touch **Done**. The pattern lock is set. The pattern will now be required to unlock the screen.

Figure 6: Pattern Selection Screen

6. Locking the Screen Using Your Fingerprint

In order to prevent unauthorized users from accessing your phone, you may wish to lock the phone using your fingerprint. On the Pixel, this feature is called Pixel Imprint. The feature can also be used to log in to some applications and make purchases. To lock the screen using Pixel Imprint:

1. Touch the bottom of any Home screen, then slide up your finger. Touch the   icon. The Settings screen appears.

2. Touch **Security**. The Security Settings screen appears.

3. Touch **Pixel Imprint**. The Unlock with Fingerprint screen appears.

4. Touch **Next**. The Unlock Selection screen appears, as shown in **Figure 7**.

5. Touch one of the following options to select a backup unlocking method:

    - **Pixel Imprint + Pattern** - Use a pattern to unlock the phone in case the phone does not recognize your fingerprint.

    - **Pixel Imprint + PIN** - Use a PIN to unlock the phone in case the phone does not recognize your fingerprint.

    - **Pixel Imprint + Password** - Use a password to unlock the phone in case the phone does not recognize your fingerprint.

    The corresponding screen appears, depending on the option that you selected.

6. Draw a pattern, enter a PIN, or enter a password. The Notifications screen appears.

7. Touch one of the following options to configure notification behavior while the phone is locked with a pattern:

    - **Show all notification content** - Displays all notifications while the phone is locked.

    - **Hide sensitive notification content** - Displays only the name of the application that sent the notification, such as Messenger or Gmail, but does not display the contents of the notification.

    - **Don't show notifications at all** - Hides all notifications while the phone is locked.

8. Touch Done. The Find the Sensor screen appears, as shown in **Figure 8**.

9. Touch the fingerprint sensor on the back of the phone. Lift your finger when the phone vibrates and touch it again. Repeat this process until the Fingerprint Added screen appears, as shown in **Figure 9**. Refer to *"Button Layout"* on page 7 to learn where the fingerprint sensor is located.

10. Touch **Done**. The Pixel Imprint setup is complete. You can now use your fingerprint to unlock the phone and to perform other actions, such as logging in to some applications and making purchases.

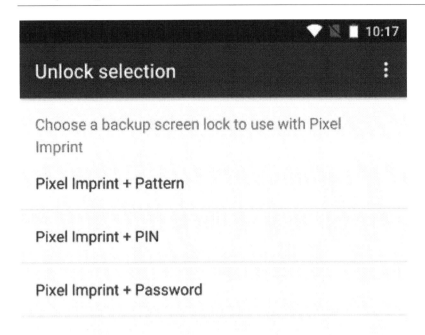

Figure 7: Unlock Selection Screen

Find the sensor

Hint: It's on the back of your phone.

NEXT

Figure 8: Find the Sensor Screen

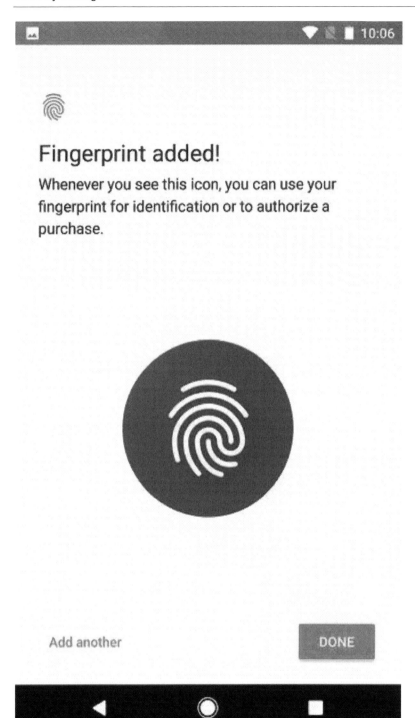

Figure 9: Fingerprint Added

7. Turning Password Visibility On or Off

When entering passwords on the phone, they can be concealed in case there is somebody else looking at the screen. Otherwise, it may be more convenient to see what is being typed. Passwords are visible by default. To turn Password Visibility on or off:

1. Touch the bottom of any Home screen, then slide up your finger. Touch the   icon. The Settings screen appears.
2. Touch **Security**. The Security Settings screen appears.
3. Touch **Make passwords visible**. The   switch appears and passwords will be visible.
4. Touch **Make passwords visible** again. The   switch appears and passwords will be concealed.

Language and Input Settings

Table of Contents

1. Selecting a Language

You can type in various languages on the phone, such as in Gmail or Messenger. You can also view all menus on the screen in a different language. To select a language:

1. Touch the bottom of any Home screen, then slide up your finger. Touch the 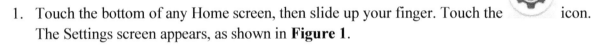 icon. The Settings screen appears, as shown in **Figure 1**.

2. Touch **Languages & input**. The Languages & Input Settings screen appears, as shown in **Figure 2**.

3. Touch **Languages**. The Language Preferences screen appears, as shown in **Figure 3**.

4. Touch **Add a language**. A list of available languages appears, as shown in **Figure 4**.

5. Touch a language in the list. The language is now available from the keyboard menu. To access the keyboard menu, touch the icon in the lower right-hand corner of the screen while using the keyboard.

To set a language as your main language for the phone, touch and hold the icon and drag the language to the first position in the list. The menu language immediately changes to the language that you selected.

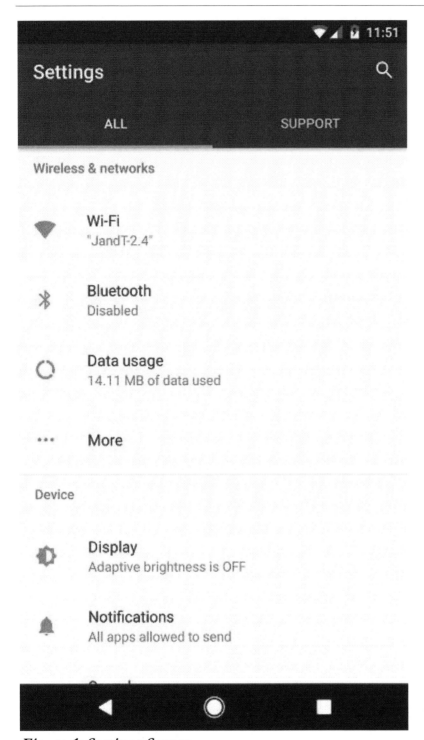

Figure 1: Settings Screen

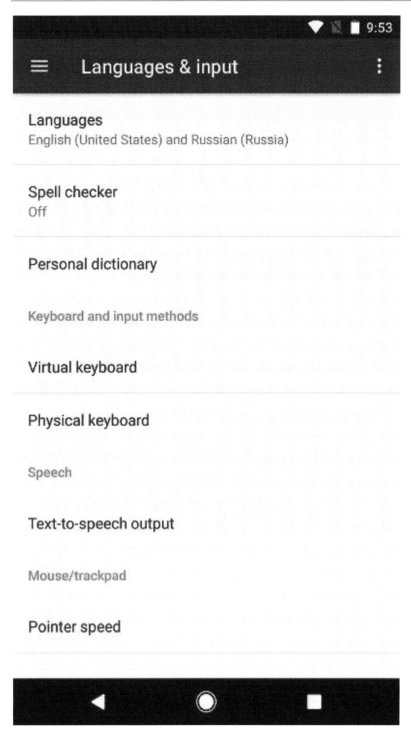

Figure 2: Languages & Input Settings Screen

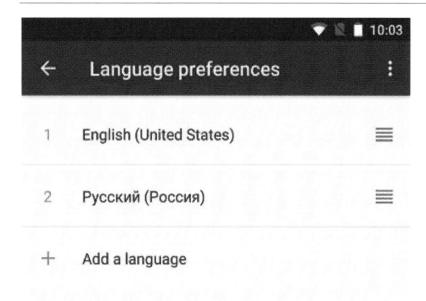

Figure 3: Language Preferences Screen

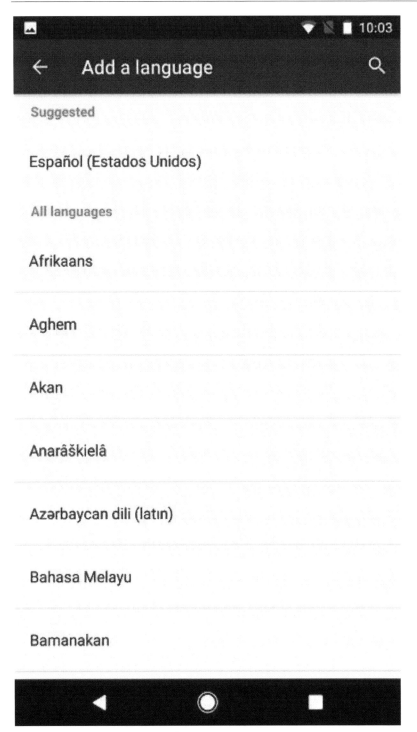

Figure 4: List of Available Languages

2. Turning Spell Checking On or Off

The phone can check the spelling of words that you type. By default, the Spell Checker is turned off. To turn Spell Checking on or off:

1. Touch the bottom of any Home screen, then slide up your finger. Touch the icon. The Settings screen appears.

2. Touch **Languages & input**. The Languages & Input Settings screen appears.

3. Touch **Spell checker**. The Spell Checker screen appears, as shown in **Figure 5**.

4. Touch **Off**. The ⬤ switch appears and the Spell Checker is turned on.

5. Touch **Off**. The ⬤ switch appears and the Spell Checker is turned off.

Figure 5: Spell Checker Screen

3. Adding Words and Phrases to the Personal Dictionary

The phone can store words in a Personal Dictionary to suggest them while you're typing. You can also add shortcuts to phrases, such as "brb" for "be right back." To add an entry to the user dictionary:

1. Touch the bottom of any Home screen, then slide up your finger. Touch the icon. The Settings screen appears.

2. Touch **Languages & input**. The Languages & Input Settings screen appears.

3. Touch **Personal dictionary**. If you have more than one language configured, touch the language for which you would like to add a personal word or phrase. The Personal Dictionary appears, as shown in **Figure 6**.

4. Touch the ✛ icon at the top of the screen. The Add to Dictionary screen appears, as shown in **Figure 7**.

5. Enter a word or phrase, and then touch **Optional shortcut**. The 'Shortcut' field is selected.

6. Enter an optional shortcut, which can be a series of letters or numbers that will be substituted with the entire word or phrase that you entered in the previous step. The shortcut is entered.

7. Touch the ⬅ button. The word or phrase and the shortcut, if any, are added to the Personal Dictionary.

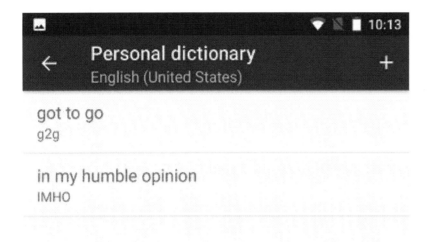

got to go
g2g

in my humble opinion
IMHO

Figure 6: Personal Dictionary

Figure 7: Add to Dictionary Screen

4. Changing the Input Method

The method that you use to input text can be changed. By default, the Android keyboard and Google voice typing are both selected. To change the text input method:

1. Touch the bottom of any Home screen, then slide up your finger. Touch the icon. The Settings screen appears.

2. Touch **Languages & input**. The Languages & Input Settings screen appears.

3. Touch **Virtual Keyboard**. The Keyboard Selection screen appears, as shown in **Figure 8**. If you have installed a third-party keyboard, such as SwiftKey, it will appear in this list.

4. Touch an input method in the list. The new input method is selected.

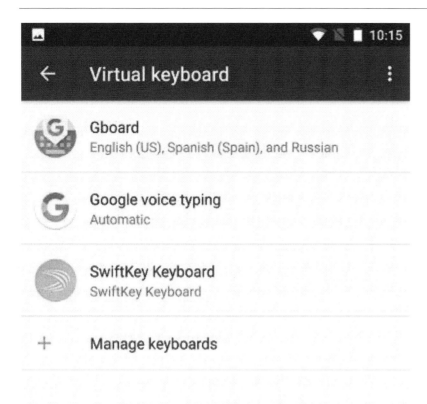

Figure 8: Keyboard Selection Screen

5. Customizing Google Assistant Settings

The Google Assistant is a voice recognition feature on the phone that can help you perform actions quickly using just your voice. The Google Assistant can be customized to improve accuracy and filter voice results. To turn on and customize the Google Assistant:

1. Touch and hold the Home button. If you have not turned on the Google Assistant, the Google Assistant dialog appears, as shown in **Figure 9**. Touch **Yes** to turn on the Google Assistant.

2. To customize the Google Assistant, touch the ⁞ icon, then touch Settings. The Google Assistant settings screen appears, as shown in **Figure 10**.

3. Touch one of the following options to customize the Google Assistant:

   - **Google Assistant** - Turns Google Assistant on or off.

   - **Use screen context** - Allows you to search for items on the screen that you are currently viewing.

   - **Assistant language** - This option is not configurable and follows the main language that you select for all phone menus. Refer to *"Selecting a Language"* on page 276 to learn how.

   - **"OK Google" Detection** - Allows you to say OK Google to launch the Voice when using the Google application, or at all times, depending on your settings. Touch Always on after touching "OK Google" Detection to leave the feature on at all times.

   - **Voice** - Select this item to configure the following options:

     o **Hands free** - Allows voice input to be provided using a Bluetooth headset or a wired headset.

     o **Speech output** - Determines whether Speech Output is always enabled or is only turned on when using a hands-free device with the phone.

     o **Offline speech recognition** - Downloads additional speech recognition languages to be used offline; touch **All** at the top of the screen to view all options.

     o **Block offensive words** - Hides offensive words when showing voice results, even if they are recognized.

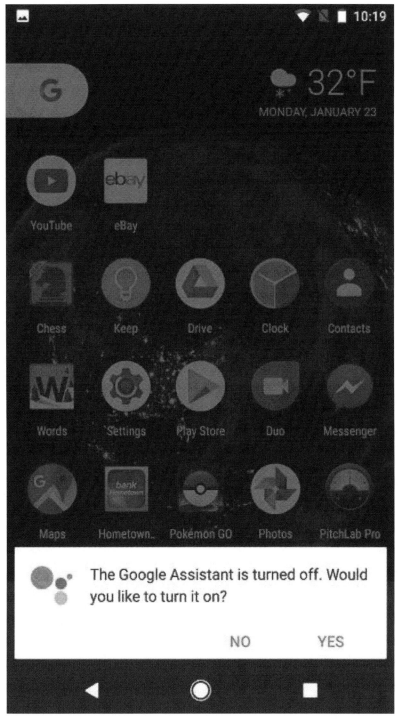

Figure 9: Google Assistant Dialog

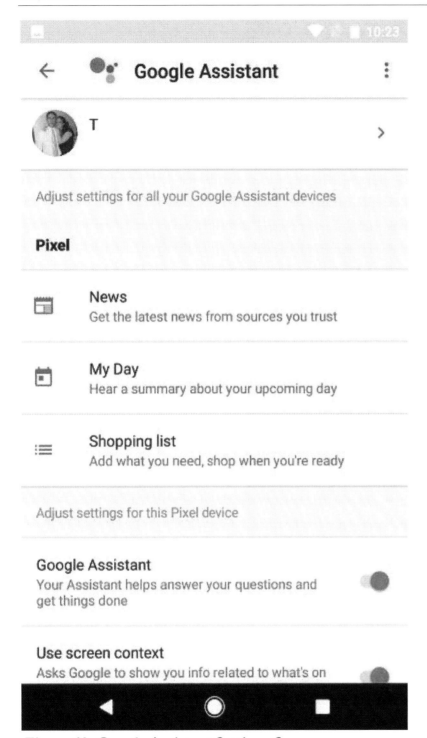

Figure 10: Google Assistant Settings Screen

6. Changing the Text-to-Speech Speaking Rate

Some applications on the phone can use the Text-to-Speech feature, which reads the text on the screen aloud. To change the speech rate of the Text-to-Speech feature:

1. Touch the bottom of any Home screen, then slide up your finger. Touch the icon. The Settings screen appears.

2. Touch **Languages & input**. The Languages & Input Settings screen appears.

3. Touch **Text-to-speech output**. The Text-to-Speech Output screen appears, as shown in **Figure 11**.

4. Move the slider next to Speech rate to the left or right to decrease or increase the speech rate, respectively. You can touch Listen to an example to get an idea of how the text-to-speech output will sound.

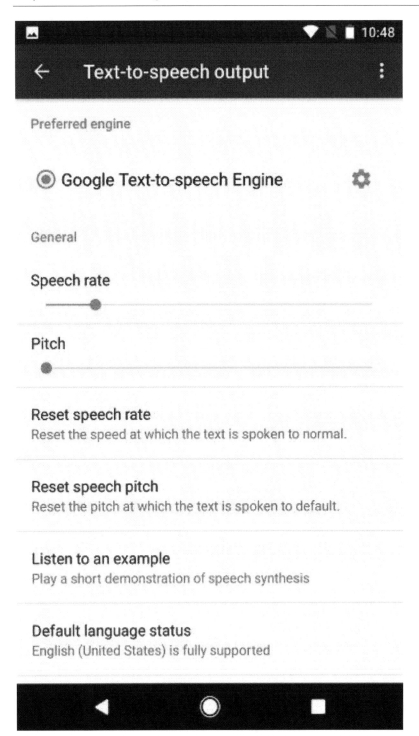

Figure 11: Text-to-Speech Output Screen

7. Downloading Additional Text-to-Speech Languages

The Text-to-Speech feature can pronounce phrases in any of five languages, including English. However, languages other than English do not come pre-installed on the phone. To download additional Text-to-Speech languages:

1. Touch the bottom of any Home screen, then slide up your finger. Touch the icon. The Settings screen appears.

2. Touch **Languages & input**. The Languages & Input Settings screen appears.

3. Touch **Text-to-speech output**. The Text-to-Speech Settings screen appears.

4. Touch the icon next to 'Google Text-to-speech Engine'. The Text-to-Speech Settings screen appears, as shown in **Figure 12**.

5. Touch **Install voice data**. A list of voice data that is available for download appears, as shown in **Figure 13**.

6. Touch the language that you want to download. The list of available voices for the language appears.

7. Touch the button next to the language that you wish to download. The corresponding Text-to-Speech language is downloaded. The button appears next to the language once it has been installed. Touch the button to uninstall the voice language.

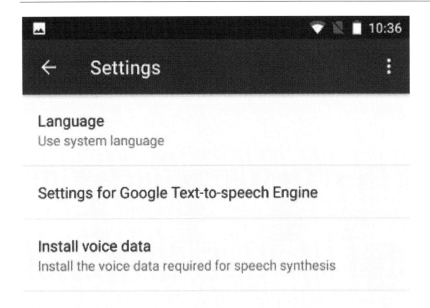

Figure 12: Text-to-Speech Settings Screen

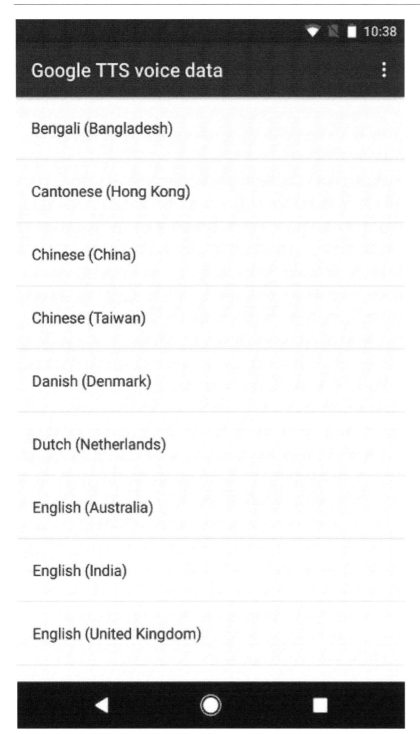

Figure 13: List of Voice Data Available for Download

Tips and Tricks

Table of Contents

1. Maximizing Battery Life

There are several things that you can do to increase the battery life of the phone:

- Lock the phone whenever it is not in use. To lock the phone, press the **Power/Sleep** button once.

- Keep the Sleep Timer set to a small amount of time before it dims and turns off the screen when the phone is idle. Refer to *"Setting the Amount of Time Before the Phone Locks Itself"* on page 251 to learn how to change the Sleep Timer.

- Turn down the brightness or turn on Automatic Brightness. Refer to *"Adjusting the Brightness"* on page 244 to learn how to change Brightness settings.

- Turn off Wi-Fi and Bluetooth when you are not using them. Refer to *"Connecting to a Wi-Fi Network"* on page 227 to learn how to turn Wi-Fi off. Refer to *"Using Bluetooth"* on page 230 to learn how to turn off Bluetooth.

- Do not use the camera, if possible. The camera uses a lot of battery power.

- Close applications that are running in the background. Refer to *"Viewing Recently Opened Applications"* on page 115 to learn how.

2. Checking the Amount of Available Memory

To check the amount of available memory at any time, touch the bottom of any Home screen, then

slide up your finger. Touch the icon. The Settings screen appears. Touch **Storage**. The available memory appears under 'Available'.

3. Freeing Up Memory

There are two actions that can free up memory on the phone: uninstalling applications and removing temporary internet files stored by the Chrome browser. Refer to *"Quickly Uninstalling Applications"* on page 298 to learn how to uninstall an application. Refer to *"Clearing the Data that is Used to Speed Up Browsing"* on page 221 to learn how to delete temporary internet files stored by Chrome.

4. Quickly Uninstalling Applications

Getting rid of applications that you no longer use will reduce clutter and free up memory. While applications may be uninstalled from Settings, this is a rather long process. To quickly uninstall an application:

1. Touch the bottom of the Home screen and slide your finger up. The Applications screen appears.
2. Touch and hold an application icon. The Home screen appears and 'Uninstall' appears at the top of the screen.
3. Drag the application icon over the word 'Uninstall'. A confirmation dialog appears.
4. Touch **OK**. The application is uninstalled.

5. Viewing the Desktop Version of a Website

By default, the Chrome browser displays mobile versions of websites. You can also view the desktop version of a website, if it is available. To view the desktop version of a website:

1. Touch the icon on the Home screen, or touch the bottom of the Home screen and slide your finger up, then touch the icon. The Chrome browser opens.

2. Navigate to a website. Refer to *"Navigating to a Website"* on page 196 to learn how.

3. Touch the icon in the upper right-hand corner of the screen. The Chrome menu appears.

4. Touch **Request desktop site**. The desktop version of the website that you are currently visiting will appear when you re-enter the URL of the current site. Some websites do not have a desktop version that is available on your mobile phone.

6. Accessing the Settings Screen Quickly

Instead of navigating through the list of applications to find the   icon, you can access the Settings screen by touching the status bar at the top of the screen and sliding your fingers down.

Then, touch the   icon. The Settings screen appears.

7. Taking Away a Website's Access to Your Location

Some websites will be able to access your location, if you allow them to do so. To take away a website's access to your location:

1. Touch the   icon on the Home screen, or touch the bottom of the Home screen and slide your finger up, then touch the   icon. The Chrome browser opens.
2. Touch the   icon in the upper right-hand corner of the browser. The Chrome menu appears.
3. Touch **Settings**. The Chrome Settings screen appears.
4. Touch **Site settings**. The Site Settings screen appears.
5. Touch **Location**. A list of previously visited websites appears. The websites that have access to your location are under the 'Allowed' list.
6. Touch a website that can access your location. The Website Settings screen appears.
7. Touch **Location access**. The Location Access menu appears.
8. Touch **Block**. Repeat steps 6 and 7 for all websites with access to your location. These websites will no longer have access to your location.

8. Clearing Notifications

You may clear all notifications at once in the Notification center. To do so, touch the status bar at the top of the screen and drag down. The Notifications center appears. Touch **Clear**. All notifications are cleared. You may also clear a single notification by touching it and sliding your finger to the left or right.

9. Using the Google Assistant

Google Assistant is a handy search assistant that responds to voice commands. To activate the Google Assistant, touch and hold the key or say **OK Google**, depending on your settings. The Google Assistant is activated and is ready to listen to your voice command. You can say commands like:

- Play Coldplay
- Watch Scandal on Netflix
- Good morning (to hear your daily briefing, including weather, meetings, news, etc.)
- Remind me to call my Mom tonight
- Set my alarm for 8am
- Will it rain tomorrow?
- Find a restaurant nearby
- "Good morning" in Chinese
- Call my wife
- Set a timer for 10 minutes
- Open YouTube
- What's on my calendar?
- Navigate to the post office
- Turn on flashlight

10. Adding a Navigation Shortcut to the Home Screen

Instead of opening the Maps application every time that you wish to navigate to an address that you often visit, add a Navigation shortcut to the Home screen. To add a Navigation shortcut:

1. Touch an empty space on a Home screen. The Home screen menu appears.
2. Touch **Widgets**. A list of available widgets appears.

3. Scroll down and touch and hold the icon. The Home screen appears.
4. Drag the shortcut to an empty space on the Home screen. The Navigation shortcut is added to the Home screen and the Create Widget screen appears.
5. Enter the address and a Shortcut name (both required), and touch **Save**. The Navigation shortcut is set up. Touch the navigation shortcut at any time to navigate to the selected address.

11. Capturing a Screenshot

To capture what is on the screen and save it as a photo, press and hold the **Volume Down** and **Power/Sleep** buttons simultaneously. Keep holding the buttons until your screen momentarily flashes a white color. The screenshot is stored in the 'Screenshot' album in the Gallery.

12. Searching the System Settings

If you are having trouble finding a particular setting, try searching the system settings. To search the settings:

1. Touch the icon on the Settings screen. The Search field appears at the top of the screen.
2. Start typing the search keywords. Matching results appear as you type.
3. Touch a result in the list to navigate to the corresponding settings screen.

13. Quickly Navigating the Settings Pages

You can quickly navigate from one settings screen to another without returning to the main Settings screen. To quickly navigate settings screens:

1. Open a settings page.
2. Touch the left-hand side of the screen and slide your finger to the right. The Settings Navigation bar appears.
3. Touch an option in the list. The corresponding settings screen appears.

14. Creating an Animated Photo

You can create an animated photo, or GIF, using the camera on the phone. To create an animated photo, touch and hold the button while using the camera. The camera captures a series of photos and automatically stores an animated photo in the photo album.

15. Performing Quick Application Actions from the Home Screen

Some applications allow you to perform quick actions right from the Home screen, such as send a message to a recent contact, search for a YouTube video, or open a new browser tab. To perform a quick action, touch and hold the application icon on the Home screen. A list of quick actions appears above or below the application icon, if quick actions are available for that application.

16. Turning the Notification Light On or Off

The Pixel has a hidden notification light, which can alert you about unread notifications or missed calls or texts. The notification light is located on the front of the phone inside the ear piece. The light is turned off by default. To turn on the notification light:

1. Touch the bottom of any Home screen, then slide up your finger. Touch the   icon. The Settings screen appears.
2. Touch **Notifications**. The Notification screen appears.
3. Touch the   icon at the top of the screen. The Configure Notifications screen appears.
4. Touch **Pulse notification light**. The Notification Light is turned on.
   Touch **Pulse notification light** again to turn it off.

17. Using Gestures to Perform Quick Actions

The Pixel allows you to perform various gestures to accomplish day-to-day tasks, such as viewing notifications or opening the camera quickly without touching the screen. To use gestures to perform quick actions:

1. Touch the bottom of any Home screen, then slide up your finger. Touch the icon. The Settings screen appears.
2. Touch **Moves**. The Moves screen appears.
3. Touch one of the following options to turn it on or off.
   - **Swipe for notifications** - Use the Fingerprint Reader on the back of the phone to view your notifications.
   - **Jump to Camera** - Open the camera by pressing the **Power/Sleep** button twice.
   - **Flip camera** - Switch between the front and rear cameras when you twist your wrist twice while holding the phone.
   - **Double-tap to check phone** - Touch the screen when it is off to check the time and notifications.
   - **Lift to check phone** - Pick up the phone to check the time and notifications.

Troubleshooting

Table of Contents

1. Phone does not turn on

Try one of the following:

- Recharge the battery using the included wall charger. If the battery power is extremely low, the screen will not turn on for several minutes. Do NOT use the USB port on your computer to charge the phone; it may not properly charge the phone.
- Replace the battery. If you purchased the phone a long time ago, you may need to replace the battery. Contact the manufacturer of your phone to learn how to replace the battery.
- Press and hold the **Power/Sleep** button for 30 seconds. The phone resets and turns back on. This is called a soft reset.

2. Phone is not responding

If the phone is frozen or is not responding, try one or more of the following. These steps solve most problems on the phone:

- **Restart the phone** - If the phone freezes while running an application, perform a soft reset by pressing and holding the **Power/Sleep** button for 30 seconds. The phone restarts.

- **Remove Media** - Some downloaded applications or music may freeze up the phone. Try deleting some of the media after restarting the phone (if you are able to access the Settings screen). Refer to *"Uninstalling an Application"* on page 109 or *"Quickly Uninstalling Applications"* on page 298 to learn how to delete an application.

- **Reset the phone** - If the above suggestions do not help, you may also reset and erase all data at once by doing the following (if you are able to access the Settings screen):

Warning: Any erased data is not recoverable.

1. Touch the bottom of any Home screen, then slide up your finger. Touch the icon. The Settings screen appears.
2. Touch **Backup & reset**. The Backup & Reset screen appears.
3. Touch **Factory data reset**. The Factory Reset screen appears.
4. Touch **Reset phone** at the bottom of the screen. A confirmation screen appears.
5. Touch **Erase Everything**. The phone is reset and all data is erased.

3. Can't surf the web

Make sure that Wi-Fi is turned on and the phone is connected to a network. Refer to *"Connecting to a Wi-Fi Network"* on page 227 to learn how to connect to a network.

If you are not in range of a Wi-Fi network, make sure that you are connected to a mobile network.

4. Screen or keyboard does not rotate

If the screen does not rotate or the full horizontal keyboard is not appearing when rotating the phone, it may be one of the following issues:

- The application does not support horizontal view.

- The phone is lying flat when rotating. Hold the phone upright for the view to change in applications that support it.

- You are viewing one of the Home screens. By default, the screen will not rotate when you are viewing a Home screen.

- Screen rotation is locked. Refer to *"Turning Automatic Screen Rotation On or Off"* on page 247 to learn how to unlock screen rotation.

5. Application does not download or install correctly

Sometimes applications may not download or install correctly. If this happens, try uninstalling and re-installing the application. Refer to *"Uninstalling an Application"* on page 109 and *"Purchasing Applications"* on page 109 to learn how.

6. Touchscreen does not respond as expected

If the touchscreen does not perform the desired functions or does not work at all, try the following:

- Remove the screen protector, if you use one.
- Make sure that your hands are clean and dry and that the touchscreen is clean. Oily fingers can make the screen dirty and unresponsive.
- Restart the phone.
- Make sure that the touchscreen does not come in contact with anything but skin. Scratches on the screen are permanent and may cause the phone to malfunction.

7. Phone is hot to the touch

When running some applications for extended periods of time, the phone may become hot. This is normal and will not harm the phone in any way.

8. Computer does not recognize the phone

If your computer does not recognize the phone, try one of the following:

- Only use the provided USB cable to connect the phone to your computer.
- Connect the phone directly to the computer instead of a USB hub.
- Make sure that the correct drivers are installed on your computer, if any are needed. If using a Mac, make sure that you have installed the Android File Transfer application. Download this application at **www.android.com/filetransfer**. Without this application, the Mac will not recognize your phone.

9. Phone does not detect a Bluetooth device

If the phone does not detect a Bluetooth device, try one of the following:

- Move the phone closer to the Bluetooth device
- Make sure that Bluetooth is enabled on the device
- Make sure that Bluetooth is enabled on the Bluetooth headset or other device

10. Microphone is Not Working

If you discover that the microphone on your Pixel is malfunctioning during a phone call, try turning the speaker phone on and off. This should turn your microphone back on.

11. What to do if you could not solve your problem

Contact Google Play Help at 855-836-3987 or check the **Google Play Help Center**.

Index

Other Books from the Author of the Help Me Series, Charles Hughes

Help Me! Guide to the Galaxy S5

Help Me! Guide to the Galaxy S4

Help Me! Guide to the Nexus 7

Help Me! Guide to the Nexus 6

Help Me! Guide to iOS 10

Help Me! Guide to the iPad Air 2

Help Me! Guide to the iPad Air

Help Me! Guide to the iPhone 7

Help Me! Guide to the iPhone 6

Help Me! Guide to the iPhone 6S

Help Me! Guide to the iPhone 5S

Help Me! Guide to the iPhone 4

Help Me! Guide to the Kindle Fire HDX

Help Me! Guide to the HTC One

Help Me! Guide to the iPod Touch

Help Me! Guide to the iPad Mini

Help Me! Guide to the Kindle Touch

Help Me! Guide to the Samsung Galaxy Note

…and many more

Made in the USA
Middletown, DE
20 January 2020